©2010 DemiDec Corporation
1002 Wall Street
Los Angeles, CA 90015

Printed in the United States of America

2010
10 9 8 7 6 5 4 3 2 1

ISBN-13: 978-1-936206-14-8

DemiDec Cram Kits may be purchased at special high-quantity discounts for use in promotions or educational purposes. Please email us for more information at contact@demidec.com, or write to DemiDec at 1002 Wall Street, Los Angeles, CA 90015.

Editorial
Dean Schaffer, Editor
Daniel Berdichevsky, Editor-in-Chief

WHAT IS A CRAM KIT?
A Word from the Editor

BETTER THAN THE TEXTBOOK YOU NEVER READ

GETTING STARTED

Everyone says that if you want to do well on an exam, cramming is not the way to do it. But not everyone has used a Cram Kit.

If you're reading this, you've already taken a big step toward improving your score. Cram Kits are DemiDec's signature study guide, focused on two types of information:

2. That which is most likely to be tested.
3. That which is most likely to be forgotten.

This Cram Kit is *not* a textbook. It does not aim to teach you everything you could ever want to know about a subject. Rather, Cram Kits give you a focused, approachable, and engaging path to success on the AP exam—especially if you're crunched for time.

So what are you waiting for? Get cramming!

Visit www.demidec.com to find out how you can Spread the Cram!

THE CRAM FAMILY

The first generation of the Cram Family delivers Cram Kits and Cram Cards in the following subjects:

AP Psychology

AP Calculus

AP Chemistry

AP Biology

SAT I

AP U.S. History

AP English Language

AP Economics (Micro and Macro)

AP Spanish Language

CRAMMING FOR SUCCESS
A Word from the Author

OVERVIEW OF THE CRAM KIT

SUMMARY

Welcome to the AP Psychology Cram Kit. Perhaps you are approaching this guide at the beginning of the school year, eager to get an edge on the competition. Or perhaps you have only a short time left before the exam and wonder how you are ever supposed to review everything. Either way, this cram kit will help you narrow your studies to cover the topics most crucial to achieving success on the AP exam.

This Cram Kit has been broken down into nine topic areas. As you can see on the chart to the right, four of these areas will require the bulk of your time. You are not expected to know the answer to every question on the exam, nor is such content mastery necessary for passing the test. However, if you know History and Research, Abnormal Behavior, Development and Personality, and Learning and Cognition, you will have covered over 60% of the material before even touching the remaining five categories.

PIECES OF THE AP PIE

- History and Research
- Biological Psychology
- Sensation and Perception
- States of Consciousness
- Learning and Cognition
- Motivation and Emotion
- Social Psychology
- Development and Personality
- Abnormal Behavior

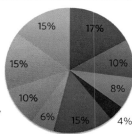

THE CLOCK IS TICKING...

If you're truly strapped for time, you can still cover a lot of ground by simply reading through the study guide and testing your knowledge of the material in the List of Lists at the end. If you have more time on your hands, try supplementing the material presented by making notes in the margins from your textbook, class lectures, and any other resources you have available.

Keep the principles of learning in mind as you study: use mnemonics; try to study for short sessions over a long period of time; study in an environment and mind frame similar to those you will be in during the exam; and create meaningful connections between the material and your personal experiences. Most of all, have fun!

CRAMMING FOR SUCCESS
How to Use This Book

A TERRIFIC TOOL	CRAMMING THE RIGHT WAY

CRAMMING FOR SUCCESS

At their best, study aids clarify troublesome concepts or processes. At their worst, they confuse.

This book strives to outline the AP Psychology curriculum in a clear and engaging manner. You've already gotten a taste of the format. Information is organized by

- Bullets, numbers, and checks
- Graphics (with pretty colors, of course)
- Tables and charts
- Bolded terms and headings

At the top of each page, you will find two headings. The larger heading, in all capital letters, refers to an overarching section or theme of the curriculum—think of it as a chapter of the book (on this page, "CRAMMING FOR SUCCESS"). The smaller heading refers to the specific topic of that page (on this page, "How to Use This Book"). These two headings will help you organize material thematically in your brain.

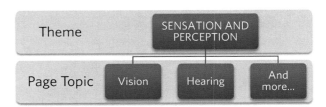

A quiz follows every page. It may cover material presented on the page previous or related information that wasn't included.

You'll find that the pages correspond to the percentages already mentioned.

CRUNCHING FOR SUCCESS

At the end of this book, you'll find a super-summary of the AP Psychology course called the Crunch Kit. Use it as a quick reference, a last-minute refresher, or a high-speed review.

Following the Crunch Kit is the List of Lists, organized by topic. These lists introduce terms and their definitions that will probably be covered on the AP Psychology exam. This section gives you a good chance to test your knowledge. Wait until you've reviewed the rest of the book and then see how many terms in the lists you can define without help. Most of the terms found in the lists are essential, so it's important to understand them fully before the test.

KNOWING WHAT'S IMPORTANT

This book will help you with the major topics in the AP Psychology course by reviewing terminology and different processes.

It's important to keep in mind that the concepts underlying the terminology are also important. For example, memorizing every psychological disorder could make you crazy. Understanding the principles behind abnormality along with the general categories of psychopathology is more important. One could say the same thing for almost every topic in AP Psychology. That doesn't mean you should ignore the details, though; just know where they come from.

THE MAJOR THEMES

In 1890, William James wrote the first psychology textbook: *Principles of Psychology*. Over 12 years, he wrote 1200 pages (be thankful I'm not so cruel). James illustrated important themes about the field as it existed then, and many of these remain true today.

- Psychology is the science of mental life
- Mental processes lead to involuntary and voluntary actions
- The brain is responsible for bodily functions
- Psychology can be studied in a variety of ways, including analysis, introspection, experimentation, and comparison
- The field includes numerous schools of thought with varying philosophical and scientific approaches

The realm of psychology is extremely vast. If it took 1200 pages to cover James' ideas in 1890, one can hardly imagine how much space it would require to truly cover all the research and ideas that have developed since then. This text by no means aims to cover all of psychology, but it does include the most important topics necessary for passing the AP exam.

READY, GET SET, STUDY!

This is an exciting time in psychology—the textbooks are changing quickly, and the field is growing and developing just as rapidly. But don't let that overwhelm you! The themes haven't changed. The mind is still an ornate structure that determines how we sense, perceive, learn, and think about the world around us—and it is still prone to error. Relate what you're studying to these concepts. This will give you the good foundation you need to tackle any AP Psychology test question. Good luck, and happy studying!

HISTORY AND RESEARCH
Psychology's Origins

A TALE OF TWO STUDIES

WHAT IS PSYCHOLOGY?

Psychology is the study of mental processes and behavior. It evolved from the joint efforts of philosophers and scientists to understand how people think and why they do the things they do.

ARMCHAIR REASONING

Socrates
- Believed that the mind and body are separate
- The mind continues on after the body dies

Plato
- Believed that humans possess innate knowledge

Aristotle
- Based theories on logic and observation
- Believed that the soul and body are not separable
- Claimed that knowledge develops based on memories and experiences

Descartes
- Believed that the mind and body are separate; the mind controls the body, and the body provides the mind with sensory information
- Thought that the mind-body interaction took place in the pineal gland
- Coined the term "reflexes" for unconscious bodily reactions to environmental stimuli

Locke
- Believed that people are born as blank slates (tabula rasa) and gain knowledge through experience

Hobbes
- Believed that the concepts of mind and soul are irrelevant
- Claimed that the brain creates consciousness

DID YOU KNOW?

The belief that the mind and body are two separate entities is known as *dualism*. Ever hear the saying mind over matter?

WILHELM WUNDT (1832-1920)

A LAB OF HIS OWN

- The founder of scientific psychology
- Trained in medicine and physiology
- Opened a psych lab in Leipzig, Germany, in 1879 to study mental processes
- Used a research technique called *introspection*, in which subjects described their reactions to stimuli
- Famous graduate students include Edward Titchener, G. Stanley Hall, James Cattell, and Lightner Witmer

STRUCTURALISM VS. FUNCTIONALISM

STRUCTURALISM

- Focused on breaking mental processes down into their fundamental components in order to understand the mind as a whole
- First psychological school of thought; developed by Wundt and Titchener
- Titchener brought psychology (and his structuralist viewpoint) to America when he left Wundt's lab to work at Cornell University

FUNCTIONALISM

- Focused on the adaptive qualities of mental processes and behaviors in order to understand what function these things serve
- William James, author of the first psychology textbook, developed this school of thought
- James was influenced by Darwin's theory of natural selection

WOMEN IN CHARGE

William James invited Mary Calkins into his Harvard psychology graduate seminar. Though she outperformed her male colleagues, Harvard refused to grant her a degree. Calkins later became the first female president of the American Psychological Association (APA) in 1905.

Margaret Floy Washburn was the first woman to be granted a doctorate in psychology (1894). She was advised by Titchener. Washburn became the second female president of the APA in 1921.

CRAM QUIZ
Psychology's Origins

QUESTION 1

Which of the following philosophers described children as blank slates?

(A) Hobbes
(B) Plato
(C) Socrates
(D) Descartes
(E) Locke

QUESTION 2

What is dualism?

(A) division of thought and behavior
(B) division of mind and body
(C) division of brain structure and function
(D) division of science and philosophy
(E) division of the schools of psychology

QUESTION 3

Who is considered the father of scientific psychology?

(A) Wundt
(B) Titchener
(C) James
(D) Locke
(E) Aristotle

QUESTION 4

What was the predominant research method of structuralism?

(A) dissection
(B) surveys
(C) naturalistic observation
(D) experimentation
(E) introspection

QUESTION 5

Who wrote *Principles of Psychology*, the first psychology textbook?

(A) Wundt
(B) Titchener
(C) Cattell
(D) James
(E) Washburn

QUESTION 6

Which of the following concepts most influenced functionalism?

(A) dualism
(B) repression
(C) natural selection
(D) self-actualization
(E) statistical validity

QUESTION 7

What is a reflex?

(A) a body movement controlled by the pineal gland
(B) a biological drive to meet survival needs
(C) a genetically predisposed sensitivity to a stimulus
(D) an involuntary response to a stimulus
(E) an unlearned species-specific behavior

QUESTION 8

Who was the first female president of the APA?

(A) Washburn
(B) Calkins
(C) Dix
(D) Ainsworth
(E) Gilligan

ANSWERS

1. E
2. B
3. A
4. E
5. D
6. C
7. D
8. B

HISTORY AND RESEARCH
Approaches to Psychology

THEORETICAL SYSTEMS

"UNDER MY UMBRELLA"

The broad field of psychology encompasses a variety of approaches and theoretical emphases.

BIOPSYCHOLOGY

- **Focus:** The relationship between physiology and behavior
- **Research Tools:** Brain imaging
- **Goals:** To determine the extent to which genetic predisposition influences behavior—the question which lies at the heart of the nature-nurture debate

BEHAVIORISM

- **Focus:** Observable behaviors, rather than unobservable mental processes; antecedents, behaviors, and consequences
- **Methods of Research:** Classical and operant conditioning
- **Famous Figures:** Pavlov, Skinner, and Watson

COGNITIVE

- **Focus:** Mental processes, such as memory, language, and problem-solving, in addition to components and purposes of thought
- **Famous Figures:** Ebbinghaus, Piaget, Loftus, and Chomsky

EVOLUTIONARY

- **Focus:** The adaptive qualities of behavior
- **Origins:** Darwin's theory of natural selection

HUMANISTIC

- **Focus:** The impact of free will and personal values on behavior
- **Famous Figures:** Maslow and Rogers

PSYCHOANALYTIC/PSYCHODYNAMIC

- **Focus:** The influence of the unconscious mind on thoughts and behaviors; the impact of childhood experiences on the development of adult personality and mental problems
- **Famous Figures:** Freud developed this theory, but Jung, Adler, and others expanded it later

GESTALT

- **Focus:** Whole experiences are more than the sum of their individual parts
- **Famous Figures:** Max Wertheimer

PROFESSIONS

FROM THEORY TO PRACTICE

Many fields of psychological research are rooted directly in the theoretical approaches. For example, biopsychology leads to biological psychologists, and cognitive psychology leads to cognitive psychologists.

TYPES OF THERAPISTS

Counseling Psychologist
- Helps people with problems related to work, school, and marriage

Clinical Psychologist
- Researches and provides therapy for people with psychological disorders

Psychiatrist
- Treats people with psychological disorders through therapy and medication
- Medical doctor

CONSULTATION

Psychologists often consult for schools and companies.

Industrial/organizational (I/O) psychologists help companies select and train employees and increase workplace morale and efficiency.

Human factors psychologists try to make products and websites more consumer-friendly.

Educational psychologists provide testing services and therapy for schoolchildren.

Psychometricians design assessments of aptitude, achievement, and personality.

CRAM QUIZ
Approaches to Psychology

QUESTION 1

Which of the following figures was a humanistic psychologist?

(A) Freud
(B) Rogers
(C) Wertheimer
(D) Watson
(E) Bandura

QUESTION 2

Which of the following types of psychologists would be most interested in defense mechanisms?

(A) cognitive
(B) behaviorist
(C) humanistic
(D) psychoanalytic
(E) evolutionary

QUESTION 3

Which theoretical perspective is espoused by a therapist who uses whichever psychological perspective is best suited to a specific patient and situation?

(A) eclectic
(B) psychodynamic
(C) humanistic
(D) cognitive-behavioral
(E) existentialist

QUESTION 4

Which of the following professionals can prescribe medications to treat psychological disorders?

(A) clinical psychologist
(B) educational psychologist
(C) counseling psychologist
(D) psychometrician
(E) psychiatrist

QUESTION 5

Which of the following types of psychologists would be most likely to use CAT scans and MRIs?

(A) behavioral
(B) biological
(C) cognitive
(D) evolutionary
(E) gestalt

QUESTION 6

What field of psychology employs the law of Pragnanz?

(A) behaviorist
(B) psychodynamic
(C) gestalt
(D) biological
(E) cognitive

QUESTION 7

Who developed the humanistic idea of self-actualization?

(A) Piaget
(B) Rogers
(C) Maslow
(D) Adler
(E) Klein

QUESTION 8

Which of the following topics is Elizabeth Loftus most famous for studying?

(A) language
(B) conditioning
(C) problem-solving
(D) repression
(E) memory

ANSWERS

1. B
2. D
3. A
4. E
5. B
6. C
7. C
8. E

HISTORY AND RESEARCH
Research Design

METHODS

DESIGN STAR

Research Type	Purpose	Strengths and Weaknesses
Experiment	Understand cause-effect relationships	- Isolates effects of independent variable - Difficult to control for confounding variables
Survey	Determine relationship between variables	- Accumulate large quantities of data quickly and inexpensively - Cannot control for confounding variables in participants' lives; people lie
Case Study	Investigate a single case in-depth	- Useful for rare circumstances or determining future research questions - Limited generalizability to others
Naturalistic Observation	Observe participants in their usual environments	- Behaviors are less influenced by observers and controlling factors - Lack of control minimizes understanding of cause-effect

EXPERIMENTS

The experimental population being studied is divided into two groups. The experimental group receives the independent variable, and the control group does not. Variables must be operationalized, meaning that whatever is being measured is clearly defined.

Independent Variable	•Variable manipulated by the researcher
Dependent Variable	•Measured response to manipulated variable
Confounding Variable	•Irrelevant variable that correlates with the independent and dependent variables

Experimental Group ➕ Control Group 🟰 Population

SAMPLING AND ASSIGNMENT

POPULATION CONTROL

Sampling is the process of choosing research participants. Assignment is the division of participants into groups. Sampling occurs before assignment.

Representative sample: The group of participants is made up of approximately the same demographics as the larger population

Random sample: Every member of the population has an equal chance of being chosen as a participant

Random assignment: Every participant has an equal chance of being placed into the experimental and control groups

Single-blind design: Participants do not know which group they are placed in; helps eliminate response bias

Double-blind design: Neither participants nor researchers know what groups participants have been assigned to; helps eliminate experimenter bias

VALIDITY AND RELIABILITY

SAY WHAT YOU MEAN, MEAN WHAT YOU SAY

Validity
•Research measures what it was intended to measure

Reliability
•Reseach can be duplicated to get the same results every time

PLACEBO EFFECT

JUST A SPOONFUL OF SUGAR

- A placebo is an inert object or procedure used to make members of the control group believe they are receiving the same treatment as the experimental group

- The placebo effect occurs when a subject's medical condition improves when she receives a placebo in the absence of other medical interventions; sometimes, thinking you are going to get better is enough to make you feel better

- Placebos are used in clinical trials of medications to determine how much of a patient's change results from the placebo effect versus the effect of the medication

CRAM QUIZ
Research Design

QUESTION 1

Which of the following types of research is most useful for determining cause and effect?

(A) correlation
(B) experiment
(C) naturalistic observation
(D) case study
(E) structured interview

QUESTION 2

Which of the following types of research is the least generalizable?

(A) case study
(B) survey
(C) experiment
(D) naturalistic observation
(E) correlation

QUESTION 3

A researcher is trying to determine the relationship between study time and test performance. What is the dependent variable?

(A) amount of time spent studying
(B) teacher's opinion of students' effort
(C) grade earned on the test
(D) amount of time spent taking the test
(E) grade earned in the class

QUESTION 4

Which of the following statistics is used to measure a test's consistency?

(A) validity
(B) standard deviation
(C) reliability
(D) correlation
(E) representativeness

QUESTION 5

Which of the following is most likely to make research participants in clinical trials feel better even though they have not received medical treatment?

(A) placebo effect
(B) demand characteristic
(C) experimenter bias
(D) iatrogenesis
(E) Hawthorne effect

QUESTION 6

What is a double-blind research design?

(A) researchers do not tell participants which group they belong to
(B) participants choose to be in either the experimental or the control group
(C) researchers randomly assign a representative sample to groups
(D) neither researchers nor participants know which participants are in which group
(E) researchers match groups based on their demographics

QUESTION 7

Which of the following predicts a relationship between two variables?

(A) theory
(B) hypothesis
(C) correlation
(D) operational definition
(E) confound

QUESTION 8

What research technique is used to minimize order effects?

(A) random assignment
(B) placebo effect
(C) stratified sampling
(D) group matching
(E) counterbalancing

ANSWERS

1. B
2. A
3. C
4. C
5. A
6. D
7. B
8. E

HISTORY AND RESEARCH
Statistics

DESCRIPTIVE STATISTICS

TELLING IT LIKE IT IS

Descriptive statistics describe a set of data without making any generalized conclusions.

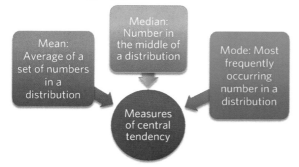

Mean: Average of a set of numbers in a distribution

Median: Number in the middle of a distribution

Mode: Most frequently occurring number in a distribution

Measures of central tendency

When a distribution is represented on a normal curve, the mean, median, and mode are the same. If the data set includes more small values than large ones, the curve is skewed to the right; if the set includes more large values than small ones, the curve is skewed to the left. (Note that the skew is based on the direction the curve tip points.) In skewed distributions, the median is more useful for describing central tendency than the mode.

EXAMPLES OF DESCRIPTIVE STATISTICS

When you get your scores back from a standardized test, you may see a **percentile rank**. A percentile tells you how you performed relative to others.

Have you ever heard that an increase in shark attacks is correlated with an increase in ice cream sales? **Correlation** is a measure of how closely related two variables are. But remember that correlation does NOT suggest causation. In the above example, both increases are a result of the warm summer season, not a causal link.

Correlations range between -1 and +1. *Positive correlation* means an increase in one variable is associated with an increase in the other. *Negative correlation* means an increase in one variable is associated with a decrease in the other. A correlation of zero means variables aren't related.

VARIABILITY

Variability describes how clustered the numbers in a data set are. The ***standard deviation*** of the data set is a measure of its variability based on the average distance between data points and the mean. If the standard deviation is low, the data is tightly clustered around the mean; if it is high, the data is loosely spread over a range of values.

INFERENTIAL STATISTICS

STATISTICAL GAMBLING

Inferential statistics are used to determine whether the results of a study on a small sample can be generalized to the larger population.

- Null hypothesis: Treatment did not have an effect in an experiment
- Alternative hypothesis: Treatment did have an effect in an experiment; a tailed alternative hypothesis states the direction of the effect
- Statistical significance: Research result was unlikely to have occurred by chance alone
- p-value: Probability of making a Type I error; commonly set at $p = .05$, meaning that the results would only occur by chance 5% of the time

TO ERROR IS HUMAN

		Real Result	
		Null hypothesis is true	Null hypothesis is false
Observed Result	Null hypo-thesis is true	Correct	**Type II error** *Conclude there is not a statistically significant difference when there is*
	Null hypo-thesis is false	**Type I error** *Conclude there is a statistically significant difference when there is not*	Correct

ETHICAL GUIDELINES

1. Institutional Review Boards (IRBs) assess research plans to determine whether they meet ethical guidelines.
2. Research participants must provide informed consent to ensure that they understand the risks and benefits of their involvement, as well as their ability to leave the study.
3. Data is often collected anonymously to ensure participants' right to confidentiality.
4. After research is completed, participants must be debriefed—the researchers explain the purpose of the study and reveal any deception used.

CRAM QUIZ
Statistics

QUESTION 1

Which of the following numbers suggests the strongest correlation?

(A) .76
(B) -.84
(C) 0
(D) .13
(E) -.49

QUESTION 2

What is indicated by a low standard deviation?

(A) Data is scattered across a wide range.
(B) Results are likely caused by chance.
(C) Data is clustered around the mean.
(D) Results are likely statistically significant.
(E) Variables have a strong linear relationship.

QUESTION 3

What is the mode of the following distribution: 8, 6, 5, 4, 1, 5, 3?

(A) 8
(B) 4
(C) 6
(D) 3
(E) 5

QUESTION 4

Which of the following is true of a Type I error?

(A) No conclusion can be made about the statistical significance of the results.
(B) The results are statistically significant.
(C) The researcher concludes that the results are not statistically significant.
(D) The null hypothesis is false.
(E) The researcher concludes that the results are statistically significant.

QUESTION 5

If there is only a 1% chance of results occurring by chance, the p-value is

(A) .01
(B) .1
(C) 1
(D) 10
(E) 100

QUESTION 6

What statistic is used to measure the distance of a score in a distribution from the mean?

(A) variability
(B) correlation coefficient
(C) z score
(D) F score
(E) regression

QUESTION 7

In a normal distribution, what percentage of scores falls within one standard deviation of the mean?

(A) 34%
(B) 68%
(C) 84%
(D) 95%
(E) 99%

QUESTION 8

Which of the following studies would be least likely to pass through an Institutional Review Board today?

(A) Milgram's obedience studies
(B) Asch's conformity studies
(C) Sherif's autokinetic effect studies
(D) Bandura's Bobo doll studies
(E) Baumrind's corporal punishment studies

ANSWERS

1. B
2. C
3. E
4. D
5. A
6. C
7. B
8. A

HISTORY AND RESEARCH
Testing and Individual Differences

THEORIES OF INTELLIGENCE

BOOK SMARTS AND STREET SMARTS

Psychologists disagree about what intelligence really is. Some perceive it as informational knowledge, while others think it is related to creativity and communication abilities.

STANFORD-BINET IQ TEST

- Alfred Binet created a test of intelligence for French schoolchildren which became the basis for IQ testing; Lewis Terman adapted Binet's test for Americans of a wider variety of ages

WECHSLER'S INTELLIGENCE SCALES

- David Wechsler developed the Wechsler Adult Intelligence Scale (WAIS) and Wechsler Intelligence Scale for Children (WISC); these are the most common modern intelligence tests

INTELLIGENCE QUOTIENT

- Originally calculated as the ratio of mental age over chronological age, multiplied by 100; now determined by comparing scores to the average scores of same-aged peers
- An IQ score of 100 is considered average; people with scores over 135 are labeled gifted; those with scores below 70 are considered mentally retarded
- The Flynn effect shows an increase in intelligence test scores over time, suggesting that tests need to be periodically renormed to keep the average for the population at 100

SPEARMAN'S GENERAL INTELLIGENCE THEORY

- Spearman argued that intelligence is a single factor, g, comprised of specific abilities, s
- He used factor analysis to determine the correlations between these specific abilities, showing that they underlie one common ability

STERNBERG'S TRIARCHIC THEORY

- Sternberg argued that there are three types of intelligence: analytical, practical, and creative

GARDNER'S MULTIPLE INTELLIGENCES

- Gardner has identified eight intelligences: linguistic, logical-mathematical, musical, spatial, kinesthetic, environmental, interpersonal, and intrapersonal

GOLEMAN'S EMOTIONAL INTELLIGENCE THEORY

- Goleman suggested that EQ is a measure of one's ability to identify and manage emotions in oneself and others

VALIDITY AND RELIABILITY REDUX

Reliability	
Test-retest reliability	Correlation of participants' scores from the same test given at two different times
Split-half reliability	Correlation of one group's scores on half a test and another groups' scores on the equivalent form of the other half

Validity	
Face validity	Test looks like it measures what it is supposed to measure
Content validity	Test measures the entire range of content it is supposed to measure
Criterion validity	Test correlates strongly with another measure of the same variables
Concurrent validity	Test correlates strongly with another previously validated test
Predictive validity	Test predicts scores on other measures of the same variables
Construct validity	Test correlates with a psychological construct

TYPES OF TESTS

Aptitude tests
- Determine abilities and potential

Achievement tests
- Determine amount of knowledge previously learned

Power tests
- Determine ability to answer questions of increasing difficulty

Speed tests
- Determine how quickly one can answer a large number of questions in an insufficient time period

PROJECTIVE TESTS

Projective Tests
Reveal personality by interpreting ambiguous stimuli

Rorschach Inkblot Test
Subjects describe what they see in a series of 10 inkblots

Thematic Aperception Test
Subjects make up stories to accompany a series of pictures

CRAM QUIZ
Testing and Individual Differences

QUESTION 1

Who devised the triarchic theory of intelligence?

(A) Spearman
(B) Sternberg
(C) Thurstone
(D) Goleman
(E) Terman

QUESTION 2

Which of the following IQ scores falls one standard deviation above the mean?

(A) 60
(B) 75
(C) 100
(D) 115
(E) 130

QUESTION 3

What kind of validity shows whether a test looks like it measures what it is supposed to measure?

(A) content validity
(B) criterion validity
(C) face validity
(D) construct validity
(E) concurrent validity

QUESTION 4

Which of the following types of tests involves interpretation of ambiguous stimuli?

(A) power tests
(B) speed tests
(C) aptitude tests
(D) achievement tests
(E) projective tests

QUESTION 5

Which of the following is not one of Gardner's eight intelligences?

(A) kinesthetic
(B) spatial
(C) musical
(D) creative
(E) linguistic

QUESTION 6

What is the heritability coefficient?

(A) proportion of individual differences that can be attributed to genetics
(B) ratio of average parental IQ over the child's IQ
(C) ratio of mental age over chronological age
(D) percentage of genes that can be passed on from parent to child
(E) proportion of genes preserved from a family's original ancestry

QUESTION 7

What is the reliability coefficient of a test that is perfectly reliable?

(A) -1
(B) 0
(C) 1
(D) 10
(E) 100

QUESTION 8

Which of the following reflects fluid intelligence?

(A) ability to use knowledge gained over time
(B) ability to solve novel problems
(C) ability to score well across several measures of intelligence
(D) ability to understand the emotions and motivations of others
(E) ability to control motor coordination

ANSWERS

1. B
2. D
3. C
4. E
5. D
6. A
7. C
8. B

BIOLOGICAL PSYCHOLOGY
Neurons to Nervous Systems

NERVOUS SYSTEM

THE GANG'S ALL HERE

Nervous System

Central Nervous System (CNS)
Brain and spinal chord
Integrative and control centers

Peripheral Nervous System (PNS)
Cranial nerves and spinal nerves
Communication lines between the CNS
and the rest of the body

Sensory (afferent) division
Somatic and visceral sensory
nerve fibers
Conducts impulses from receptors
to the CNS

Motor (efferent) division
Motor nerve fibers
Conducts impulses from the CNS
to effectors (muscles and glands)

Somatic nervous system
Somatic motor (voluntary)
Conducts impulses from the
CNS to skeletal muscles

Autonomic nervous system (ANS)
Visceral motor (involuntary)
Conducts impulses from the CNS to cardiac
muscles, smooth muscles, and glands

Parasympathetic division
Conserves energy
Promotes "housekeeping"
functions during rest

Sympathetic division
Mobilizes body systems during
activty ("fight or flight")

NEURON

BRANCHING OUT

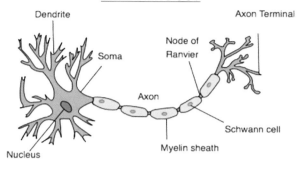

The nervous system is composed of nerves, which are bundles of neurons. The cell body of the neuron is the *soma*; it contains the nucleus. *Dendrites* branch out from the soma and receive input from other neurons. The *axon* responds to messages from the dendrites and soma, transmitting information to other cells through a long, tubular structure. Axons are often coated with a *myelin sheath* made up of *Schwann cells*; this insulation speeds up neural impulses. The *nodes of Ranvier* are the gaps in the sheath. At the end of the axon, *terminal buttons* branch out to other cells. The gap between the terminal buttons and the other cell bodies is the *synapse*.

NEURAL TRANSMISSION

MIND THE GAP

Action potential: Nerve impulse carrying a message within and between cells; triggered by a certain threshold of stimulation; electricity travels within cells, and chemicals (neurotransmitters) travel between them.

All or none principle: If the threshold of excitation is passed, the neuron will fire with a fixed strength.

Refractory phase: Immediately after the neuron fires, no amount of stimulation will cause it to fire again; then, for a short period, the neuron will require more stimulation than usual to fire.

Neurotransmitters: Chemical messengers that can be excitatory, causing a neuron to fire, or inhibitory, stopping a cell from firing; neurotransmitters that have finished passing along their messages can be broken down by enzymes or absorbed back into the original cell through reuptake; examples of neurotransmitters include acetylcholine, serotonin, dopamine, norepinephrine, GAPA, and endorphins.

CRAM QUIZ
Neurons to Nervous Systems

QUESTION 1

What part of the neuron insulates the axon and speeds up neural impulses?

(A) dendrites
(B) myelin sheath
(C) terminal buttons
(D) synapse
(E) nodes of Ranvier

QUESTION 2

What principle explains the fixed strength of nerve impulses?

(A) threshold of excitation principle
(B) absolute refractory principle
(C) ion stimulation principle
(D) all or none principle
(E) cell membrane permeability principle

QUESTION 3

What part of the nervous system is directly responsible for the fight-or-flight reaction?

(A) peripheral nervous system
(B) sympathetic nervous system
(C) parasympathetic nervous system
(D) somatic nervous system
(E) autonomic nervous system

QUESTION 4

What part of the nervous system is directly responsible for the heart and digestive tract?

(A) peripheral nervous system
(B) sympathetic nervous system
(C) parasympathetic nervous system
(D) somatic nervous system
(E) autonomic nervous system

QUESTION 5

What types of neurons convey sensory information to the brain?

(A) efferent neurons
(B) interneurons
(C) association neurons
(D) afferent neurons
(E) multipolar neurons

QUESTION 6

Through what process are neurotransmitters absorbed back into the cells from which they were released?

(A) action potential
(B) enzymatic decomposition
(C) reuptake
(D) dendrite binding
(E) synaptic decay

QUESTION 7

Who discovered that the nervous system is made up of individual neurons?

(A) Sperry
(B) Cajal
(C) Wernicke
(D) Gazzaniga
(E) Darwin

QUESTION 8

What part of the nervous system is responsible for conserving energy?

(A) peripheral nervous system
(B) sympathetic nervous system
(C) parasympathetic nervous system
(D) somatic nervous system
(E) autonomic nervous system

ANSWERS

1. B
2. D
3. B
4. E
5. D
6. C
7. B
8. C

BIOLOGICAL PSYCHOLOGY
Brain Structures and Imaging

NEUROANATOMY

PUTTING YOUR BEST BRAIN FORWARD

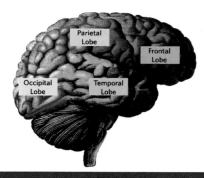

Hindbrain

- Oldest part of the brain
- Structures in top of the spinal cord
- Controls basic biological functions
- Cerebellum: muscle movements, balance
- Medulla Oblongata: breathing, digestion, heart rate, blood pressure, swallowing
- Reticular Activating System: wakefulness and alertness
- Pons: passes information between regions of the brain
- Thalamus: conveys information between visual and auditory systems

Midbrain/Limbic System

- Second oldest part of the brain
- Structures between spinal cord and forebrain
- Integrates muscle movements and sensory information
- Hippocampus: memory formation
- Amygdala: anger and frustration
- Hypothalamus: temperature, hunger and thirst, sexual arousal, endocrine system

Forebrain/Cerebral Cortex

- Most recent part of the brain
- Outer layer of the brain
- Involved in higher level cognitive functions
- Left and right hemispheres joined by corpus callosum; people with corpus callosum severed are considered split-brain patients
- Left hemisphere controls language processing; Broca's area is responsible for speaking ability; Wernicke's area is responsible for speech comprehension
- Frontal lobe: executive functions, reasoning and judgment
- Parietal lobe: touch, pressure, texture, pain, temperature
- Temporal lobe: auditory input
- Occipital lobe: visual input

NEUROIMAGING

BETTER THAN X-RAY VISION

Brain imaging techniques allow researchers to see the structures and functions of varying regions of the brain.

	EEGs use electrodes on the scalp to amplify and record the electrical activity of neurons in the brain. They can identify the electrical waves produced by specific behaviors.
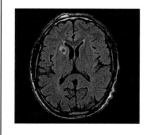	MRIs use magnetic fields and radio waves to create pictures of the brain. fMRIs show activity in the brain by taking scans in succession and comparing the amount of blood flow to see what parts of the brain are most active.
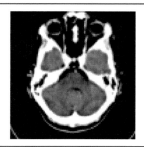	CT (or CAT) scans build a picture of the brain with a series of X rays. All of the sliced images are put together to create a 3-D representation.
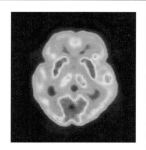	PET scans detect the movement of glucose in the brain during the performance of a task. They can locate where the most glucose is consumed to determine what parts of the brain are involved in specific behaviors.

CRAM QUIZ
Brain Structures and Imaging

QUESTION 1

What imaging technique uses glucose levels to determine what structures of the brain are most active?

(A) EEG
(B) fMRI
(C) MRI
(D) CAT
(E) PET

QUESTION 2

Which of the following disorders is incorrectly matched with its characteristic symptom?

(A) Broca's aphasia: impaired language comprehension
(B) agnosia: impaired ability to recognize sensory stimuli
(C) apraxia: impaired ability to organize purposeful movements
(D) alexia: impaired reading ability
(E) dysgraphia: impaired writing ability

QUESTION 3

What imaging technique uses electrodes on the head to monitor electrical activity of the regions of the brain?

(A) EEG
(B) fMRI
(C) MRI
(D) CAT
(E) PET

QUESTION 4

What is the brain's primary fuel?

(A) deoxyribose
(B) fructose
(C) glucose
(D) neuraminic acid
(E) saccharic acid

QUESTION 5

Which of the following brain structures developed most recently?

(A) cerebral cortex
(B) hippocampus
(C) cerebellum
(D) pons
(E) hypothalamus

QUESTION 6

Which of the following brain structures joins the left and right hemispheres together?

(A) cerebral cortex
(B) corpus callosum
(C) optic chiasma
(D) ventromedial hypothalamus
(E) reticular activating system

QUESTION 7

Which of the following brain structures is not part of the limbic system?

(A) hippocampus
(B) amygdala
(C) lateral hypothalamus
(D) ventromedial hypothalamus
(E) medulla oblongata

QUESTION 8

Which of the following topics does Michael Gazzaniga research?

(A) neural transmission
(B) evolutionary brain development
(C) neurotransmitters
(D) split-brain patients
(E) regulation of body arousal

ANSWERS

1. E
2. A
3. A
4. C
5. A
6. B
7. E
8. D

BIOLOGICAL PSYCHOLOGY
Anatomy and Genetics

ENDOCRINE SYSTEM

SACK OF HORMONES

Major Endocrine Glands
Male   Female

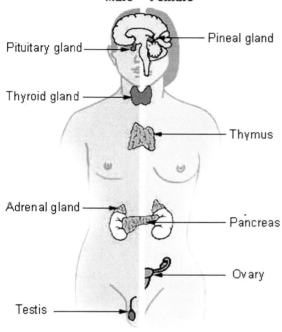

- Pituitary gland
- Pineal gland
- Thyroid gland
- Thymus
- Adrenal gland
- Pancreas
- Ovary
- Testis

The endocrine system sends information around the body through groups of cells called glands. Glands release hormones.

Structure	Function
Pituitary gland	Triggers other glands to release hormones
Adrenal gland	Regulates stress; causes fight-or-flight response
Pineal gland	Controls wake/sleep cycle and seasonal functions
Thyroid gland	Regulates the body's metabolism
Pancreas	Produces insulin
Ovaries	Produce estrogen
Testes	Produce testosterone

GENETICS

SWIMMING IN THE GENE POOL

Humans have 46 chromosomes. Half of these come from each parent. Chromosomes are made up of DNA; segments of DNA, called genes, determine traits.

Dominant trait	• Requires only one copy of the gene to be expressed
Recessive trait	• Requires two copies of the gene to be expressed
Genotype	• An individual's genetic makeup or blueprint
Phenotype	• An individual's outward appearance

GENETIC DISORDERS

Genetic disorders may result from chromosomal abnormalities in the body cells and sex cells.

Down syndrome is caused by an extra chromosome in the 21st pair; it often results in mental retardation.

Huntington's disease results from degeneration of the basal ganglia and causes muscle impairment.

Turner's syndrome results when a baby is born with a single X chromosome, instead of the usual XX or XY combinations; *Klinefelter's syndrome* results from an extra X chromosome (XXY). These disorders can impair sexual development.

TWINS

IT TAKES TWO

Identical (monozygotic) twins develop from a single fertilized egg and share 100% of their genetic material.

Fraternal (dizygotic) twins develop from two independently fertilized eggs that were implanted simultaneously. They are not identical and do not have the same genetic makeup.

Scientists researching the nature-nurture debate often study twins who have been raised together by their biological families as well as those raised apart by adoptive families to determine the extent of genetic influence on an individual's behavior.

CRAM QUIZ
Anatomy and Genetics

QUESTION 1

Which of the following hormones is secreted by the pituitary gland in order to stimulate the adrenal glands in stressful situations?

(A) adrenocorticotropic hormone
(B) epinephrine
(C) norepinephrine
(D) thyroxine
(E) testosterone

QUESTION 2

What part of the endocrine system controls the body's metabolism?

(A) pituitary gland
(B) pineal gland
(C) pancreas
(D) adrenal gland
(E) thyroid gland

QUESTION 3

How many chromosomes does a person typically inherit from his or her mother?

(A) 7
(B) 13
(C) 23
(D) 46
(E) 92

QUESTION 4

	A	a
A	AA	Aa
a	Aa	aa

If A is a dominant normal gene and a is a recessive gene for a disease, what is the probability of the child being a healthy carrier of the disease?

(A) 0%
(B) 25%
(C) 50%
(D) 75%
(E) 100%

QUESTION 5

Which of the following disorders is characterized by an extra X chromosome?

(A) Tay-sachs disease
(B) Turner's syndrome
(C) Klinefelter's syndrome
(D) Parkinson's disease
(E) Down syndrome

QUESTION 6

An individual with mental retardation, a rounded face, short fingers, and slanted eyes likely suffers from

(A) Huntington's disease
(B) Gaucher's disease
(C) Turner's syndrome
(D) Down syndrome
(E) Tay-sachs disease

QUESTION 7

What percentage of genetic material do monozygotic twins share?

(A) 10%
(B) 25%
(C) 50%
(D) 75%
(E) 100%

QUESTION 8

What is the term for an individual's genetic blueprint?

(A) trait
(B) Punnett square
(C) heritability
(D) genotype
(E) phenotype

ANSWERS

1. A
2. E
3. C
4. C
5. C
6. D
7. E
8. D

SENSATION AND PERCEPTION
Vision

VISUAL SENSATION

LET THE SUNSHINE IN

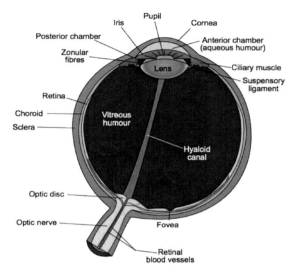

1. The eye gathers light reflected off of objects. Different wavelengths of light are perceived as different colors.
2. Light enters the eye through the cornea, which helps protect the outer eye and focus the light.
3. The light then passes through the pupil, which is controlled by the iris. The pupil dilates and contracts to determine how much light passes through.
4. Through accommodation, the curvature of the lens changes to focus light. At this point, images are flipped upside down and mirrored.
5. The image is projected onto the retina in the back of the eye. When light activates the neurons in the retina, it is known as transduction. The retinal cells include rods and cones. Rods are responsible for black and white vision and peripheral vision. Cones are responsible for color vision; they are primarily located in the fovea (the center of the retina).
6. When the information passes from the retina to the occipital lobe, it goes through the optic nerves, where there is a blind spot with no rods or cones. The optic nerves cross at the optic chiasma; at this point, the visual information goes from each side of the eye to the opposite side of the brain.
7. The visual cortex of the brain receives the information. At this point, sensation changes to perception.

VISUAL STIMULI

DISTAL VS. PROXIMAL STIMULI

The *distal stimulus* is the object being perceived as it exists in the environment. The *proximal stimulus* is the image of the object as it is projected on the retina.

FIGURE-GROUND RELATIONSHIP

What do you see in this picture?
A vase? Two faces?

The visual field is divided into foreground and background. Perception allows the viewer to distinguish objects from their surroundings, but a single stimulus can sometimes be seen in multiple ways.

THEORIES OF COLOR VISION

TRICHROMATIC

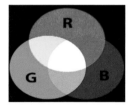

According to the Young-Helmholtz trichromatic theory, the eye has receptors for each of the primary colors of light: red, green, and blue. Stimulating different combinations of cones causes the eye to perceive other colors. (Note that these primary colors differ from those of pigment: red, *yellow*, and blue.)

OPPONENT PROCESS

The opponent process theory suggests that cells are stimulated and inhibited by opposite colors. Opposing colors are red and green, yellow and blue, and white and black. When you stare at one color for awhile and then look at a white background, you should see its opposing color—this is called an afterimage.

CRAM QUIZ
Vision

QUESTION 1

Which of the following colors would a person with dichromatic color blindness have the least difficulty seeing?

(A) red
(B) green
(C) black
(D) yellow
(E) blue

QUESTION 2

Hubel and Wiesel discovered that neurons in the visual cortex differentiate visual images such as lines, curves, and motion. What are these neurons called?

(A) prototype stimulators
(B) schema activators
(C) feature detectors
(D) sensory coders
(E) discrimination cells

QUESTION 3

Where are the cones of the eye located?

(A) cornea
(B) iris
(C) optic chiasma
(D) pupil
(E) fovea

QUESTION 4

What are the primary colors of light?

(A) red, blue, yellow
(B) white, black, gray
(C) red, blue, green
(D) red, yellow, green
(E) white, black, blue

QUESTION 5

What part of the eye is responsible for peripheral vision?

(A) rods
(B) cones
(C) retina
(D) lens
(E) cornea

QUESTION 6

What is a distal stimulus?

(A) an object that can be perceived with use of binocular and monocular cues
(B) an object located in the foreground
(C) an object's sensory information converted into neural signals
(D) an object as it exists in its environment
(E) an image of an object projected on the retina

QUESTION 7

If you stare at a blue dot and then look away at a white piece of paper, what color afterimage will you see?

(A) yellow
(B) green
(C) red
(D) blue
(E) black

QUESTION 8

What process translates sensory stimuli into neural signals?

(A) accommodation
(B) transduction
(C) dilation
(D) contralateral shift
(E) assimilation

ANSWERS

1. C
2. C
3. E
4. C
5. A
6. D
7. A
8. B

SENSATION AND PERCEPTION
Vision

GESTALT PRINCIPLES

LAW OF PRAGNANZ

People tend to perceive objects in a simple and orderly way.

○ ○ ○ ○ ○ ○ ○ ○	*Proximity*: Objects located close together are perceived as being part of the same group
(dashed circle and square)	*Closure*: The mind fills in gaps in recognizable objects in order to make them complete
○ ○ ○ ○ ● ● ● ●	*Similarity*: Objects that appear similar are perceived as being part of the same group
(cross/plus shape)	*Continuity*: Objects that form a continuous visual pattern are perceived as being part of the same group

PERCEPTUAL PROCESSING

BOTTOM-UP VS. TOP-DOWN

Bottom-up processing involves breaking an object down into its parts. It is also called *feature analysis* because the feature detectors in the brain recognize the different elements of the objects. These components are built together into the overall image.

Top-down processing uses prior experiences to identify objects. Schemata are mental representations of the world based on experience; they can create perceptual sets, which predispose people to view the world in a certain way. Perceptual sets can influence top-down processing, which is faster (but less accurate) than bottom-up processing.

THE CAT

The second letter of each of these words is ambiguously shaped. Experience allows us to read "the cat," but breaking up the elements of these words would not allow us to identify them.

DEPTH PERCEPTION

BINOCULAR CUES

Binocular cues rely on two eyes set apart on the face, each seeing images from a different angle.

- Retinal disparity: The more similar the images each eye sees, the farther away the object is. Large disparities between the images suggest that the object is close.
- Convergence: The eyes turn inward based on the closeness of the object they are viewing. The closer the object, the more inward they turn. The brain uses the angle at which the eyes are turned to gauge distance.

MONOCULAR CUES

Monocular cues rely on one eye gauging distance independently.

- Linear perspective: Parallel lines appear to converge in the distance
- Interposition: Objects that block the view of other objects appear closer
- Relative size: Objects that are farther away project smaller images on the retina than closer objects
- Texture gradient: Detailed textures are apparent close up, but they appear dense from a distance
- Relative clarity: Objects that appear blurry and unclear look farther away than those that are crisp and easy to see
- Motion parallax: Distant objects appear to move slowly and in the same direction as the viewer, while close objects seem to move quickly and in the opposite direction as the viewer

PERCEPTION AND CULTURE

MULLER-LYER ILLUSION

"Carpentered" cultures that use many right angles see the top lines as having different lengths. Cultures that do not have as many right angles and corners can usually see that the lines are the same length.

CRAM QUIZ
Vision

QUESTION 1

When a series of lights turn on and off in succession at a steady rate, they cause an effect known as the

(A) Phi phenomenon
(B) Motion parallax
(C) Autokinetic effect
(D) Stroboscopic effect
(E) Optical flow

QUESTION 2

Which of the following researchers studied the development of depth perception using the visual cliff?

(A) Sherif
(B) Asch
(C) Weber
(D) Gibson
(E) Wiesel

QUESTION 3

Which of the following is not a monocular cue to depth perception?

(A) Interposition
(B) Convergence
(C) Relative clarity
(D) Motion parallax
(E) Linear perspective

QUESTION 4

On what does top-down processing rely most?

(A) Feature analysis
(B) Prototypes
(C) Signal detection
(D) Threshold detection
(E) Experience

QUESTION 5

Which of the following is not included in the law of pragnanz?

(A) Texture
(B) Similarity
(C) Proximity
(D) Continuity
(E) Closure

QUESTION 6

Which of the following monocular cues indicates that an object is close by?

(A) The object looks extremely different from one eye to the other.
(B) The object is blocked from view by another object.
(C) The object does not appear crisp.
(D) The object appears to move slowly in the same direction as the viewer.
(E) The object appears to have detailed textures.

QUESTION 7

According to the law of similarity, when are objects grouped together?

(A) When they are located close together
(B) When they form a continuous visual pattern
(C) When they look alike
(D) When they have gaps that can be filled by the mind
(E) When they move in the same direction

QUESTION 8

What effect explains why still lights appear to move in the darkness?

(A) phi phenomenon
(B) motion parallax
(C) autokinetic effect
(D) stroboscopic effect
(E) optical flow

ANSWERS

1. A
2. D
3. B
4. E
5. A
6. E
7. C
8. C

SENSATION AND PERCEPTION
Hearing

AUDITORY SENSATION

CAN YOU HEAR ME NOW?

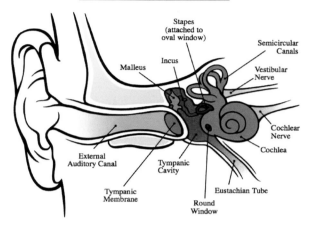

1. Sound waves enter the ear through the outer ear, or pinna.
2. The waves travel through the ear canal until they reach the eardrum, or tympanic membrane, which vibrates when hit by the waves.
3. The eardrum is attached to three bones called the ossicles; individually, they are the hammer (malleus), anvil (incus), and stirrup (stapes). The vibration passes through these bones to the oval window.
4. The oval window passes the vibration on to the cochlea, which is located in the basilar membrane and the organ of Corti.
5. The sound waves are then transferred to the auditory nerve and into the temporal lobe.

AMPLITUDE AND FREQUENCY

The *amplitude* of sound waves is their height. It determines their loudness and is measured in decibels.

The *frequency* of the waves is a measure of their length. It determines their pitch and is measured in megahertz. High frequency is associated with high pitch and densely packed waves. Low frequency is associated with low pitch and loosely packed waves.

PITCH THEORIES

PLACE VS. FREQUNCY

Frequency Theory
The hair cells in the cochlea fire at different frequencies. Low pitched sounds can be sensed by the rate of firing.

Place Theory
Sound waves are generated at different locations in the cochlea. High and low pitches depend on which hair cells vibrate.

DEAFNESS

Conduction Deafness

- Results from damage to the middle or outer ear
- The problem occurs before sound is conducted to the cochlea

Sensorineural Deafness

- Also known as nerve deafness
- Results from damage to the cochlea or auditory cortex
- When hair cells degenerate, they will not regrow
- Can be caused by loud noises

CRAM QUIZ
Hearing

QUESTION 1

Which of the following controls the decibel level of sound waves?

(A) amplitude
(B) frequency
(C) pitch
(D) vibration location
(E) transduction

QUESTION 2

What is the collective name for the hammer, anvil, and stirrup?

(A) tympanic membrane
(B) ossicles
(C) cochlea
(D) organ of Corti
(E) basilar membrane

QUESTION 3

What part of the ear is responsible for balance?

(A) incus
(B) cochlea
(C) vestibular sacs
(D) eardrum
(E) malleus

QUESTION 4

Which of the following is caused by damage to the outer or middle ears?

(A) sensorineural deafness
(B) tinnitus
(C) otitis externa
(D) conductive deafness
(E) nerve deafness

QUESTION 5

What is the highest frequency humans can hear?

(A) 20 Hz
(B) 200 Hz
(C) 2,000 Hz
(D) 20,000 Hz
(E) 200,000 Hz

QUESTION 6

Which structure is the beginning of the inner ear?

(A) tympanic membrane
(B) ossicles
(C) organ of Corti
(D) vestibular sacs
(E) oval window

QUESTION 7

Which of the following statements is true according to the volley principle?

(A) Receptor cells have a fixed firing capacity.
(B) Receptor cells alternate firing.
(C) Receptor cells decrease their firing intensity over time.
(D) Receptor cells fire simultaneously.
(E) Receptor cells generate lengthy pulses

QUESTION 8

Why is sensorineural deafness harder to treat than conduction deafness?

(A) It involves permanent hair cell destruction.
(B) It is caused by genetics.
(C) It destroys the brain's ability to comprehend noise.
(D) It involves permanent eardrum destruction.
(E) It occurs before language skills are learned.

ANSWERS

1. A
2. B
3. C
4. D
5. D
6. E
7. B
8. A

SENSATION AND PERCEPTION
Senses, Thresholds, and Attention

TOUCH, TASTE, SMELL, AND BODY SENSES

BEYOND THE SIXTH SENSE

TOUCH
- Skin has cutaneous and tactile receptors, which provide information about pressure, pain, and temperature
- Pressure and movement receptor cells are myelinated; pain and temperature receptor cells are not myelinated
- Different areas of the body have varying numbers of nerve endings; for example, the fingertips are more sensitive to touch than the elbow
- Pain serves as a warning system to prevent injury
- According to the gate-control theory of pain, high priority messages temporarily shut the gate on low priority messages; if you rub your hand after smashing it against something, the pain will be reduced by the rubbing sensation

TASTE/GUSTATION
- The tongue is covered in bumps called papillae, which contain the taste buds
- The basic tastes are sweet, salty, bitter, and sour
- People have varying levels of sensitivity to taste; densely packed taste buds lead to stronger taste
- Flavor is a combination of taste and smell

SMELL/OLFACTORY
- Chemical molecules in the air are drawn into the nose, where they reach the mucous membrane
- Up to 100 kinds of receptor cells absorb smells and send the sensory information directly to the limbic system

VESTIBULAR
- This sense informs the body of its orientation and balance
- Canals in the inner ear contain fluid; when the head moves, the fluid moves; the sensors then alert the brain of where the body is
- If the fluid moves around a lot, the individual may experience dizziness

KINESTHETIC
- This sense gives the brain information about where specific body parts are located
- The muscles and joints keep track of where all the body parts are and how they are oriented

THRESHOLDS

MAKING A DIFFERENCE

Detection	Discrimination
Absolute threshold Minimal amount of stimulation necessary to detect stimulus at least half the time	**Just noticeable difference** Minimum distance between stimuli necessary to detect them as distinct
Signal detection theory There are four potential outcomes in a detection trial: hit, miss, false alarm, and correct rejection	**Weber's law** The difference threshold is proportional to the intensity of the stimulus

HABITUATION

CH-CH-CHANGES

Habituation: Decreased response to a stimulus after repeated exposure for a period of time; this is a primarily unconscious process, but the stimulus can still be detected if the subject is asked to pay attention to it.

Dishabituation: A slight change in the stimulus causes it to be noticeable again.

Sensory adaptation: Unconscious change in the sensory system's response to a stimulus; the senses tire out after constant exposure to the stimulus; this change cannot be controlled like habituation.

ATTENTION

GETTING NOTICED

Attention is the processing of a limited amount of information taken out of the massive amount brought in by all the senses.

Selective attention involves focusing on one thing while ignoring another. The cocktail party phenomenon exemplifies this type: while talking in a noisy room, one can still usually hear his name mentioned in another conversation; though the person is consciously focusing on his own conversation, he is still filtering information from the rest of the room.

Divided attention involves attempting to focus on multiple things simultaneously. This is increasingly difficult when the stimuli being focused on activate the same sense.

CRAM QUIZ
Senses, Thresholds, Attention

QUESTION 1

Who proposed the filter theory of selective attention?

- (A) Broadbent
- (B) Weber
- (C) Fechner
- (D) Hubel
- (E) Wiesel

QUESTION 2

Which of the following is not a potential outcome of signal detection theory?

- (A) hit
- (B) miss
- (C) bias
- (D) false alarm
- (E) correct rejection

QUESTION 3

The vestibular sense receives information from the

- (A) muscles
- (B) joints
- (C) outer ear
- (D) inner ear
- (E) papillae

QUESTION 4

A research participant performs a dichotomous listening task, hearing a different message in each ear. The participant is asked to repeat one of the messages; this is known as

- (A) filtering
- (B) shadowing
- (C) allocating
- (D) resourcing
- (E) echoing

QUESTION 5

Who founded the field of psychophysics?

- (A) Broadbent
- (B) Weber
- (C) Fechner
- (D) Hubel
- (E) Wiesel

QUESTION 6

The body's ability to stop noticing the sensation of clothing on the body can be attributed to

- (A) habituation
- (B) dishabituation
- (C) sensory adaptation
- (D) selective attention
- (E) divided attention

QUESTION 7

Which of the following stimuli would require the greatest change in intensity for the difference between stimuli to be noticeable?

- (A) faint scent
- (B) light-weight object
- (C) soft touch
- (D) subtle taste
- (E) loud noise

QUESTION 8

Which of the following topics would not be studied in the field of parapsychology?

- (A) clairvoyance
- (B) psychokinesis
- (C) telepathy
- (D) precognition
- (E) kinesthesis

ANSWERS

1. A
2. C
3. D
4. B
5. C
6. A
7. E
8. E

STATES OF CONSCIOUSNESS
Sleep and Dreaming

SLEEP STAGES

TO SLEEP, PERCHANCE TO DREAM

Sleep is an altered state of consciousness typically occurring in darkness and following a roughly 24-hour day-to-night pattern governed by the circadian rhythm. Sleep is divided into stages based on brain waves, as measured by EEGs; each sleep cycle lasts about an hour and a half.

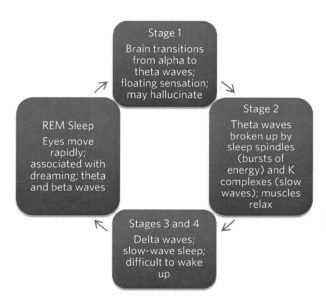

Stage 1
Brain transitions from alpha to theta waves; floating sensation; may hallucinate

Stage 2
Theta waves broken up by sleep spindles (bursts of energy) and K complexes (slow waves); muscles relax

Stages 3 and 4
Delta waves; slow-wave sleep; difficult to wake up

REM Sleep
Eyes move rapidly; associated with dreaming; theta and beta waves

REBOUND

When people are deprived of REM sleep, they have more frequent and lengthier periods of it the next time their bodies are allowed to sleep normally. Lengthy sleep deprivation can cause a variety of psychological and physical symptoms, including memory loss, hallucinations, dizziness, and muscle pain.

DREAMS

Dreaming is primarily associated with REM sleep, but it can occur during other stages of sleep, as well. Dreams are typically studied through self-reports.

Freud believed that the literal content of dreams underlies an unconscious meaning made up of symbols.

According to the *activation-synthesis theory*, dreams explain what is happening to the body during REM sleep. The *information-processing theory* suggests that dreams are related to experiences that occurred during the preceding day.

LEVELS OF CONSCIOUSNESS

DOWN THE RABBIT HOLE

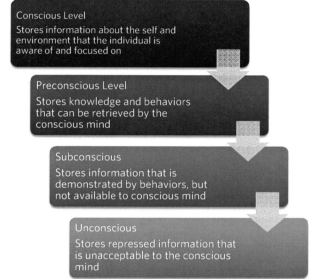

Conscious Level
Stores information about the self and environment that the individual is aware of and focused on

Preconscious Level
Stores knowledge and behaviors that can be retrieved by the conscious mind

Subconscious
Stores information that is demonstrated by behaviors, but not available to conscious mind

Unconscious
Stores repressed information that is unacceptable to the conscious mind

SLEEP DISORDERS

WHAT DREAMS MAY COME

Insomnia: Persistent difficulty falling or staying asleep; one of the most common sleep disorders, it can be caused by stress, substance abuse, inconsistent sleep patterns, and exercise before bedtime.

Narcolepsy: Inability to stay awake; patients may fall asleep suddenly, usually for about five minutes and often at inappropriate times; individuals typically fall straight into REM sleep; its exact cause is unknown, but it may result from the lack of a neurotransmitter called hypocretin, which is responsible for alertness.

Sleep apnea: Patients repeatedly stop breathing for short periods of time throughout the night; it interferes with deep sleep; obesity increases one's risk for it.

Somnambulism: The patient wanders around, sometimes performing other activities, while asleep; it usually occurs within the first few hours of falling asleep and lasts for 15 seconds to 30 minutes at a time; the patient may wake up or go back to bed without remembering the incident.

Night terrors: Extreme fear during stage four sleep; breathing and heart rate accelerate; the individual may move around and talk, suggesting a connection with sleepwalking; patients rarely wake up during the episode or remember it after; most common among children.

CRAM QUIZ
Sleep and Dreaming

QUESTION 1

A few hours after falling asleep, a six-year-old sits up in bed screaming and then falls back asleep. The next day, he does not remember waking up or why he was scared. From which of the following sleep disorders does he most likely suffer?

(A) sleep apnea
(B) night terrors
(C) somnambulism
(D) insomnia
(E) narcolepsy

QUESTION 2

What primary characteristic distinguishes the stages of sleep?

(A) time of night
(B) amount of time asleep
(C) muscle tone
(D) brain wave activity
(E) presence of dreams

QUESTION 3

Which of the following theories suggests that dreams are a byproduct of what is occurring to the body during sleep?

(A) activation-synthesis
(B) information-processing
(C) REM rebound
(D) latent content
(E) manifest content

QUESTION 4

What level of consciousness contains retrievable information of which the individual is not presently aware?

(A) conscious
(B) preconscious
(C) nonconscious
(D) subconscious
(E) unconscious

QUESTION 5

Which stage of sleep is characterized by sleep spindles?

(A) REM sleep
(B) stage 1
(C) stage 2
(D) stage 3
(E) stage 4

QUESTION 6

Which stage of sleep is also known as paradoxical sleep?

(A) REM sleep
(B) stage 1
(C) stage 2
(D) stage 3
(E) stage 4

QUESTION 7

You get into a car accident with a woman who has fallen asleep at the wheel. She claims that she cannot control when she falls asleep and that she often does so at inopportune times. From which of the following sleep disorders does she most likely suffer?

(A) sleep apnea
(B) night terrors
(C) somnambulism
(D) insomnia
(E) narcolepsy

QUESTION 8

How long is the average sleep cycle?

(A) 30 minutes
(B) 60 minutes
(C) 90 minutes
(D) 120 minutes
(E) 180 minutes

ANSWERS

1. B
2. D
3. A
4. B
5. C
6. A
7. E
8. C

STATES OF CONSCIOUSNESS
Drugs and Hypnosis

DRUGS

THE MAGIC PILL

Drug	Effect	Example
Depressants	- Diminish neural activity and slow down body functions - Impair memory and judgment - Diminish pain and anxiety - Slow breathing, constrict pupils, cause lethargy	- Alcohol - Barbiturates - Opiates
Stimulants	- Excite neural activity and speed up body functions - Keep the body awake - Diminish appetite - Increase heart and breathing rates, raise blood sugar, cause pupils to dilate - Some cause increased energy and euphoria while others may result in anxiety and irritability	- Caffeine - Nicotine - Amphetamines - Ecstasy - Methamphetamine - Cocaine
Analgesics	- Dull senses - Relieve pain - Can diminish the body's ability to produce natural endorphins	- Heroin - Morphine - Codeine - Demerol - Vicodin - Oxycodone
Hallucinogens	- Distort sensory perceptions and create imaginary sensory experiences - May cause paranoia - Also known as psychedelics	- Marijuana - LSD - Ecstasy

SUBSTANCE ABUSE AND DEPENDENCE

TRIED TO MAKE ME GO TO REHAB

Substance Abuse
Distress or impairment in functioning as a result of substance use

Substance Dependence
Physical and psychological reliance on a drug that results from chronic drug abuse
Characterized by tolerance and withdrawal

Tolerance
Need more of a substance to achieve the same effect

Withdrawal
Symptoms that occur as a result of stopping substance use

HYPNOSIS

COUNTING BACKWARDS

10. Hypnosis is an altered state of consciousness characterized by vivid imagined experiences
9. Ernest Hilgard suggested the neodissociative theory, which states that the mind is divided into two parts; one part follows the hypnotic suggestions, and the other is a hidden observer
8. Posthypnotic suggestions are instructions given during hypnosis to be followed after leaving the trance
7. Posthypnotic amnesia is the forgetting of what occurred while hypnotized
6. Role theory claims that hypnotized people act as they are expected to
5. State theory posits that hypnosis alters awareness of the environment
4. Some people are more easily hypnotized than others
3. Hypnosis has been used clinically to extract childhood memories, though the authenticity of these memories is controversial
2. Posthypnotic suggestion has been used to treat pain, stress, and addiction
1. People in a trance state are relaxed and easily persuaded

CRAM QUIZ
Drugs and Hypnosis

QUESTION 1

Which of the following drugs is not classified as an analgesic?

(A) heroin
(B) morphine
(C) amphetamines
(D) Demerol
(E) Vicodin

QUESTION 2

Which of the following drugs is a depressant?

(A) nicotine
(B) cocaine
(C) caffeine
(D) alcohol
(E) LSD

QUESTION 3

When an individual continues to use drugs despite negative physical and psychological consequences, his behavior is best described as

(A) abuse
(B) tolerance
(C) withdrawal
(D) addiction
(E) dependence

QUESTION 4

Drugs that act like neurotransmitters are called

(A) agonists
(B) antagonists
(C) catalysts
(D) reuptakers
(E) receptors

QUESTION 5

A chronic smoker is hypnotized and told to stop smoking when she exits the trance. This is an example of

(A) posthypnotic amnesia
(B) posthypnotic suggestion
(C) dissociation
(D) state theory
(E) role theory

QUESTION 6

Which theory of hypnosis was espoused by Ernest Hilgard?

(A) neodissociative theory
(B) state theory
(C) role theory
(D) neurohypnotism theory
(E) hypnotherapy

QUESTION 7

Which of the following is not an effect of stimulants?

(A) pupil dilation
(B) increased heart rate
(C) increased blood sugar level
(D) diminished appetite
(E) slow breathing

QUESTION 8

Hallucinogens are also known as

(A) anxiolytics
(B) psychedelics
(C) psychotics
(D) hypnotics
(E) narcotics

ANSWERS

1. C
2. D
3. E
4. A
5. B
6. A
7. E
8. B

LEARNING AND COGNITION
Classical Conditioning

STIMULUS AND RESPONSE

PAVLOV'S DOGS

When people think of classical conditioning, they think of Russian physiologist Ivan Pavlov. While studying digestion, Pavlov discovered that dogs could pair the tone of a bell with the presence of food. The dogs began to salivate at the presence of the bell alone.

The unconditioned stimulus produces an involuntary response. Food, for example, causes salivation. Food, then, is the unconditioned stimulus, and salivation is the unconditioned response.

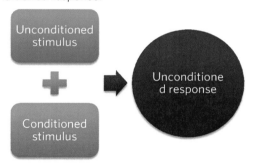

When the unconditioned stimulus of food is joined with a neutral stimulus, such as a bell, the two become paired together to produce salivation.

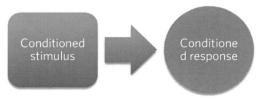

Ultimately the neutral stimulus can produce salivation on its own, making it a conditioned stimulus and the salivation a conditioned response.

PAIRING METHODS

BACKWARDS AND FORWARDS

Forward conditioning: Conditioned stimulus is presented before the unconditioned stimulus (most effective).

- *Delay conditioning*: Conditioned stimulus remains present until the unconditioned stimulus begins.
- *Trace conditioning*: Conditioned stimulus is removed before the presentation of the unconditioned stimulus.

Simultaneous conditioning: Conditioned stimulus and unconditioned stimulus are presented at the same time.

Backward conditioning: Unconditioned stimulus is presented before the conditioned stimulus (least effective).

TERMS AND CONDITIONS

THE FINE PRINT

Anything that can be learned can be unlearned. *Acquisition* results when the conditioned stimulus can produce the conditioned response without the presence of the unconditioned stimulus. However, if the conditioned stimulus is repeatedly presented without the unconditioned stimulus, the association between the two will diminish, and *extinction* will occur. If the response does happen to reappear after it has been extinguished, it is called *spontaneous recovery*.

 Much of learning is trial and error. When subjects respond to stimuli that are similar to the conditioned stimuli, it is known as *generalization*. When the subjects have been taught to tell the difference between the closely related stimuli, it is considered *discrimination*.

The pattern of acquisition can begin all over again. When a conditioned stimulus is used as an unconditioned stimulus, it can produce a new response. This is called higher-order or *second-order conditioning*. For example, if a bell that prompts salivation is paired with a flashing light, the light could begin to prompt salivation all on its own, as well.

CRAM QUIZ
Classical Conditioning

QUESTION 1

When a previously conditioned stimulus is used as an unconditioned stimulus, it is known as
- (A) higher-order conditioning
- (B) trace conditioning
- (C) backward conditioning
- (D) delay conditioning
- (E) simultaneous conditioning

QUESTION 2

What type of conditioning is exemplified when the conditioned stimulus is present until the unconditioned stimulus begins?
- (A) higher-order conditioning
- (B) trace conditioning
- (C) backward conditioning
- (D) delay conditioning
- (E) simultaneous conditioning

QUESTION 3

A group of dogs have been trained to sit whenever they hear any bell ring. One dog, though, will only sit when he hears the bell he was trained with. What does this exemplify?
- (A) acquisition
- (B) generalization
- (C) discrimination
- (D) extinction
- (E) second-order conditioning

QUESTION 4

Which of the following types of classical conditioning is least effective?
- (A) higher-order conditioning
- (B) trace conditioning
- (C) backward conditioning
- (D) delay conditioning
- (E) simultaneous conditioning

QUESTION 5

A young girl is afraid of fluffy, white rabbits. Fear of which of the following stimuli would demonstrate generalization?
- (A) loud noises
- (B) giraffes
- (C) rabbit food
- (D) white cats
- (E) lights

QUESTION 6

How can a learned behavior be extinguished?
- (A) The unconditioned stimulus is repeatedly presented without the conditioned response.
- (B) The conditioned stimulus is repeatedly presented without the unconditioned stimulus.
- (C) The conditioned stimulus is repeatedly presented without the unconditioned response.
- (D) The unconditioned stimulus is repeatedly presented without the unconditioned response.
- (E) The conditioned stimulus is repeatedly presented without the conditioned response.

QUESTION 7

What kind of conditioning includes delay and trace conditioning?
- (A) simultaneous conditioning
- (B) higher-order conditioning
- (C) aversive conditioning
- (D) backward conditioning
- (E) forward conditioning

QUESTION 8

In the case of Pavlov's dogs, what was the conditioned stimulus?
- (A) a bell
- (B) food
- (C) salivation
- (D) light
- (E) licking

ANSWERS

1. A
2. D
3. C
4. C
5. D
6. B
7. E
8. A

LEARNING AND COGNITION
Classical Conditioning (Continued)

LITTLE ALBERT

AW, RATS!

John Watson and Rosalie Rayner demonstrated classical conditioning in the Little Albert experiment: they tested a little boy named Albert and determined that he was not afraid of small animals but *was* afraid of loud noises.

The researchers repeatedly presented Albert with a white rat while simultaneously making the loud noise that Albert feared. Albert would become upset by the noise, and soon by the presentation of the rat alone. Albert had been conditioned to fear rats.

He then began to generalize this fear to other white, fluffy things. Watson had planned to recondition Albert, but never had the opportunity—Albert's mother took him away before the experiment could be finished.

CASE STUDY BREAKDOWN

- Loud noise = Unconditioned stimulus
- Rat = Conditioned stimulus
- Fear/crying = Unconditioned and conditioned response
- Rat and noise presented at same time = Simultaneous conditioning
- Fear of other white objects = Generalization
- Distinguishing rat from similar stimuli = Discrimination
- Pairing of loud noise and rat = Acquisition
- Presenting rat without loud noise = Extinction
- Fear of the white rat after extinction = Spontaneous recovery

TASTE AVERSION

THE (CHERRY) GARCIA EFFECT

Aversive conditioning attaches unpleasant stimuli to undesired behaviors to create a negative association.

John Garcia discovered *conditioned taste aversion.* He found that rats in radiation chambers would no longer drink water from the plastic bottles in the chambers because they associated the water with the nausea caused by the radiation.

People, too, are likely to attach illness to food or drink. Let's say you have a stomach bug, but don't realize it. You eat some Cherry Garcia ice cream for a snack. Soon after, you vomit. The stomach bug is the true cause of your illness, but you blame it on the ice cream and never eat it again.

This effect is easy to condition and hard to extinguish. It can be very useful, though. If an alcoholic takes a drug that makes him feel sick every time he drinks, it may help him quit drinking. If a nail-biter's nail polish makes her ill, it could get her to stop biting.

APPROACHES TO CLASSICAL CONDITIONING

CONTIGUITY VS. CONTINGENCY

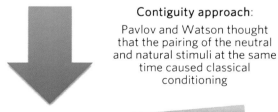

Contiguity approach:
Pavlov and Watson thought that the pairing of the neutral and natural stimuli at the same time caused classical conditioning

Contingency approach:
Robert Rescorla suggested the association between the neutral and natural stimuli occurs because the conditioned stimulus *predicts* the unconditioned stimulus

CRAM QUIZ
Classical Conditioning

QUESTION 1

Prior to the Little Albert experiment, Albert was most afraid of
- (A) bright lights
- (B) loud noises
- (C) small animals
- (D) large vehicles
- (E) foul smells

QUESTION 5

An animal is most likely to associate illness with
- (A) noise
- (B) light
- (C) food
- (D) germs
- (E) exercise

QUESTION 2

What kind of conditioning was used in the Little Albert experiment?
- (A) forward conditioning
- (B) delay conditioning
- (C) trace conditioning
- (D) simultaneous conditioning
- (E) backward conditioning

QUESTION 6

Why does Robert Rescorla believe classical conditioning works?
- (A) The conditioned stimulus occurs at the same time as the unconditioned stimulus.
- (B) The conditioned stimulus predicts the unconditioned stimulus.
- (C) The conditioned stimulus predicts the conditioned response.
- (D) The conditioned stimulus occurs at the same time as the conditioned response.
- (E) The conditioned stimulus is generalized to other stimuli.

QUESTION 3

In the Little Albert experiment, what was the conditioned stimulus?
- (A) rat
- (B) noise
- (C) fear
- (D) Watson
- (E) fluffy things

QUESTION 7

What approach to classical conditioning did Pavlov and Watson espouse?
- (A) contingency approach
- (B) reinforcement approach
- (C) generalization approach
- (D) aversive approach
- (E) contiguity approach

QUESTION 4

Who discovered conditioned taste aversion?
- (A) Watson
- (B) Rayner
- (C) Pavlov
- (D) Skinner
- (E) Garcia

QUESTION 8

What school of psychology did Watson establish?
- (A) humanistic
- (B) cognitive
- (C) behaviorism
- (D) functionalism
- (E) gestalt

ANSWERS

1. B
2. D
3. A
4. E
5. C
6. B
7. E
8. C

LEARNING AND COGNITION
Operant Conditioning

REINFORCEMENT

PETE AND REPEAT

Every behavior has consequences. Operant conditioning involves learning a response in order to obtain a reward or avoid a punishment.

THORNDIKE'S LAW OF EFFECT

Edward Thorndike was one of the first operant conditioning researchers. He studied hungry cats in puzzle boxes. The amount of time required for the cats to get out of the boxes to the food located nearby decreased with each attempt. Thorndike suggested that the cats were strengthening the connection between stimulus and response.

Thorndike's *law of effect* states that the likelihood of repeating a behavior increases if the consequences are pleasant, while the likelihood decreases if the consequences are unpleasant.

Reinforcement

Positive reinforcement: Reward that increases the likelihood of repeating a response

Negative reinforcement: Removal of an aversive stimulus that increases the likelihood of repeating a response

Punishment

Positive punishment: Aversive stimulus is administered to decrease the likelihood of repeating a response

Negative (omission) punishment: Reward is withheld to decrease the likelihood of repeating a response

TYPES OF REINFORCERS

- Primary reinforcement: Naturally satisfying reinforcers that do not need to be learned, such as food and water
- Secondary reinforcement: Learned reinforcers, such as money, that come to be associated with behaviors

SCHEDULES OF REINFORCEMENT

KEEPING THE TRAINS ON TIME

Continuous	•Reward every correct response •Learning and extinction occur quickly
Intermittent	•Not all correct responses are rewarded •Learning and extinction occur slowly
Fixed-ratio	•Reward after a preset number of responses
Variable-ratio	•Reward after an unpredictable number of responses
Fixed-interval	•Reward after a preset period of time
Variable-interval	•Reward after an unpredictable period of time

THE SKINNER BOX

GOOD THINGS COME IN SMALL PACKAGES

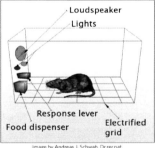

Skinner Box
- Loudspeaker
- Lights
- Response lever
- Food dispenser
- Electrified grid

Image by Andreas J. Schwab, Dr.rer.nat. Assoc. Professor, McGill University

B.F. Skinner was another pioneer in the study of operant conditioning (in fact, he coined the term). He designed an apparatus commonly called a Skinner Box or operant conditioning chamber. He would place rats inside the box, which contained a lever and a food dispenser. When the rats pressed the lever, they received food. The food positively reinforced pressing the lever.

Additional research with operant conditioning chambers has utilized electric shocks, loud noises, and lights. If the rats press the lever to terminate the shock or noise, they are demonstrating negative reinforcement. If the rats are shocked when they press the lever, the researchers are employing positive punishment. If food is taken away when the rats press the lever, it exemplifies negative punishment. Lights are sometimes used to alert the rats to the presence of food.

CRAM QUIZ
Operant Conditioning

QUESTION 1

A rat is rewarded for going near a lever. Then it is rewarded for touching the lever. Finally, the rat is rewarded for the desired behavior: pressing down on the lever. What does this scenario exemplify?

- (A) secondary reinforcement
- (B) fixed-ratio reinforcement
- (C) omission training
- (D) insight learning
- (E) shaping

QUESTION 2

Which of the following is NOT a primary reinforcer?

- (A) food
- (B) water
- (C) money
- (D) air
- (E) sex

QUESTION 3

Mary works at a fast food restaurant and receives a paycheck every other week. What reinforcement schedule does this reward exemplify?

- (A) fixed-interval
- (B) fixed-ratio
- (C) variable-interval
- (D) variable-ratio
- (E) continuous

QUESTION 4

A second grade teacher gives his students gold star stickers when they perform desired behaviors. At the end of each week, students with five or more gold stars can pick out a toy or candy. This is an example of a(n)

- (A) differential reinforcement of successive approximations
- (B) continuous reinforcement schedule
- (C) contingency approach
- (D) token economy
- (E) variable-interval schedule

QUESTION 5

A dog is shocked every time it tries to escape from a cage. After a number of attempts, the dog gives up and stops trying to escape. What is this called?

- (A) negative reinforcement
- (B) learned helplessness
- (C) conditioned resistance
- (D) response deprivation
- (E) conditioned depression

QUESTION 6

When an animal refuses to perform a conditioned behavior that goes against its nature, it is known as

- (A) learned helplessness
- (B) shaping
- (C) instinctual drift
- (D) stimulus resistance
- (E) reflexive priority

QUESTION 7

Which of the following is an example of positive punishment?

- (A) A teenager has his TV taken away for breaking curfew.
- (B) A worker makes an annoying noise go away by pressing a button.
- (C) A dog is given a treat for sitting when told.
- (D) A handler is bitten when he pets a frightened bird.
- (E) A diner is refused food service when he enters a restaurant without shoes or a shirt.

QUESTION 8

Who developed the law of effect?

- (A) Thorndike
- (B) Skinner
- (C) Pavlov
- (D) Watson
- (E) Garcia

ANSWERS

1. E
2. C
3. A
4. D
5. B
6. C
7. D
8. A

LEARNING AND COGNITION
Other Methods of Learning

OBSERVATIONAL AND LATENT LEARNING

MONKEY SEE, MONKEY DO

Observational learning goes by a number of names. These include modeling, social learning, and vicarious learning. It occurs when individuals learn how to do something by watching and imitating others.

Bobo Doll

People often wonder if children who see violence will act more violently themselves. Albert Bandura explored this issue by having children watch videos of adults playing with toys, including Bobo dolls. In some videos, adults aggressively beat up the dolls, while others played non-aggressively. The children were later given a chance to play in a room full of toys, again including Bobo dolls. Those children who observed aggressive behaviors tended to attack the dolls while those who saw the nonaggressive adults did not usually act aggressively.

RAT RACE

Edward Tolman's Rats		
Group 1	**Group 2**	**Group 3**
Received a reward every time they completed a maze; they steadily learned how to run the maze faster	Did not receive any reward for maze completion; their performance did not improve much	Received no reward for the first half of the trials but was rewarded during the second half; at first, performance did not change much, but it improved drastically in the second half

Latent learning involves hidden knowledge that becomes apparent once reinforcement is provided. Some behaviors have to be worth your while. For example, Edward Tolman discovered that rats could create cognitive maps of mazes, but they would not run the mazes quickly until they were rewarded.

INSIGHT LEARNING

THE "AHA!" MOMENT

Insight learning occurs through sudden realization of how to solve a problem—it is that "Eureka!" or "Aha!" moment when the light bulb goes on over your head.

Wolfgang Kohler studied insight learning in chimpanzees. In one study, Kohler put the chimps in rooms with bananas hanging overhead, out of reach. The room contained several boxes, but a single box alone was not tall enough to reach the bananas. After considerable frustration, the chimps would suddenly pile the boxes up on top of each other and climb to get to the bananas. They seemed to have a spontaneous understanding of how to get to their food.

ABSTRACT LEARNING

THE BIG PICTURE

Abstract learning involves understanding concepts, which are rules for organizing stimuli into groups.

Researchers presented pigeons with pictures. Some showed trees and some did not. The pigeons were taught to peck for food when shown a picture of a tree. The pigeons would peck even when presented with images of trees that they had never seen before. This behavior suggests that the pigeons did not simply memorize specific images—they understood the concept of trees.

Similar studies suggest that pigeons understand the concepts of *same* and *different*. The pigeons were presented with shapes; when given the choice between multiple shapes, some pigeons learned to peck for the shape that was the same as the original shape while others learned to peck at the different shape.

CRAM QUIZ
Other Methods of Learning

QUESTION 1

What kind of learning did Wolfgang Kohler study?
(A) observational learning
(B) operant conditioning
(C) insight learning
(D) abstract learning
(E) latent learning

QUESTION 2

Which of the following researchers studied observational learning?
(A) Bandura
(B) Tolman
(C) Kohler
(D) Skinner
(E) Thorndike

QUESTION 3

Bandura used Bobo dolls to study
(A) playing styles
(B) imagination
(C) parental modeling
(D) conditioned inhibition
(E) aggressive behavior

QUESTION 4

Which of the following groups of rats would be the slowest to learn the path through a maze?
(A) rats that receive no rewards for maze completion
(B) rats that receive a reward every time they complete a maze
(C) rats that only receive rewards for the first half of maze trials
(D) rats that only receive rewards for the second half of maze trials
(E) rats that receive a reward every other time they complex a maze

QUESTION 5

A chimpanzee is put in a cage with bananas outside it. The chimp has a short and a long stick, but neither one alone can reach the bananas. The chimp realizes that it must connect the sticks to get to the bananas. What does this process exemplify?
(A) observational learning
(B) latent learning
(C) classical conditioning
(D) abstract learning
(E) insight learning

QUESTION 6

According to Donald Hebb, how does learning occur?
(A) Neurons form and strengthen connections with each other.
(B) Concepts are used to organize stimuli into groups.
(C) Positive behaviors are reinforced with rewards.
(D) Neutral stimuli are associated with involuntary responses.
(E) Sudden realizations bring about solutions to problems.

QUESTION 7

A child observes an adult engaging in violent behavior. The child is most likely to
(A) fear aggression
(B) act aggressively
(C) act non-aggressively
(D) act the same as he would have, regardless of seeing the adult
(E) reprimand the adult

QUESTION 8

Which of the following researchers would be most likely to study the biological factors of learning?
(A) Rescorla
(B) Ross
(C) Premack
(D) Kandel
(E) Kohler

ANSWERS

1. C
2. A
3. E
4. A
5. E
6. A
7. B
8. D

LEARNING AND COGNITION
Memory

SHORT-TERM TO LONG-TERM

LET THE MEMORY LIVE AGAIN

Stages of memory processing

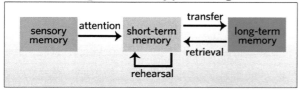

Short-term Memory

- Holds information for about 30 seconds
- Can hold about seven items (plus or minus two)
- Chunking is a method of grouping information together so that more can be remembered
- Information is kept through maintenance (repetition) and elaborative (comprehension) rehearsal
- Storage is best for the first and last few items in a list (serial position effect)

Working Memory

- Used for short-term active procesing of information
- Information is held in the brain and manipulated
- Needed for problem-solving

Long-term Memory

- Can store encoded information permanently
- Includes episodic memory (such as personal life events), semantic memory (which includes general knowledge), and procedural memory (behavioral skills)
- Memory is state-dependent, meaning that it is recalled better in the same situation as it was encoded
- Flashbulb memory is a vivid memory of an emotional event

SENSORY MEMORY

ECHOES OF ICONS

George Sperling discovered that people could hold incoming sensory information perfectly in their memory for a brief period of time. *Iconic memory* is a photographic image of visual information; it lasts for less than a second. *Echoic memory* holds auditory information for about three seconds. The sensory information is quickly replaced by new stimuli.

FORGETTING

FADE AWAY

Information can be lost naturally through decay if it is not used, but it can be relearned faster than when it was learned originally. Memory can also be lost through interference, which occurs as a result of competing information, and amnesia, which is typically caused by brain injury or psychological trauma.

Retroactive Interference	• New information interferes with the ability to recall old information
Proactive Interference	• Old information interferes with the ability to recall recently learned information
Retrograde Amnesia	• Loss of memory for information prior to an event
Anterograde Amnesia	• Inability to remember new information after an event
Source Amnesia	• Inability to remember where information came from

CRAM QUIZ
Memory

QUESTION 1

On average, how much information can be held in short-term memory?

(A) 3 items
(B) 7 items
(C) 10 items
(D) 12 items
(E) 14 items

QUESTION 2

Your parents can remember exactly where they were and what they were doing when President Kennedy was assassinated. This is an example of

(A) episodic memory
(B) semantic memory
(C) procedural memory
(D) flashbulb memory
(E) state-dependent memory

QUESTION 3

Joe experienced an upsetting breakup while studying for a test, causing him to be extremely upset. While taking the test, he continued to feel upset, which helped him to remember the information. This is an example of

(A) episodic memory
(B) semantic memory
(C) procedural memory
(D) flashbulb memory
(E) state-dependent memory

QUESTION 4

Amy got in a car accident and hit her head hard against the steering wheel. Afterward, she had difficulty remembering personal information and general knowledge but still knew how to do things like tie her shoes and ride her bike. Which kind of memory remained intact?

(A) episodic memory
(B) semantic memory
(C) procedural memory
(D) flashbulb memory
(E) state-dependent memory

QUESTION 5

Which of the following researchers studied sensory memory?

(A) Sperling
(B) Loftus
(C) Luria
(D) Chomsky
(E) Whorf

QUESTION 6

Which of the following types of forgetting most likely occurs as a result of brain injury?

(A) decay
(B) retroactive interference
(C) proactive interference
(D) amnesia
(E) reconstruction

QUESTION 7

Banana, monkey, tree, bird, cave, waterfall, dirt, swim, fly

In the above list, which item would be most difficult to recall given the serial position effect?

(A) banana
(B) monkey
(C) bird
(D) swim
(E) fly

QUESTION 8

Which of the following researchers studied reconstructed memory?

(A) Sperling
(B) Loftus
(C) Luria
(D) Chomsky
(E) Whorf

ANSWERS

1. B
2. D
3. E
4. C
5. A
6. D
7. C
8. B

LEARNING AND COGNITION
Language and Creativity

LANGUAGE ELEMENTS AND GRAMMAR

BUILDING BLOCKS

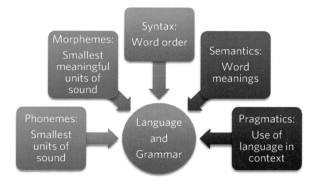

TRANSFORMERS

Noam Chomsky believed that language is organized according to transformational grammar, which is divided into surface structure and deep structure.

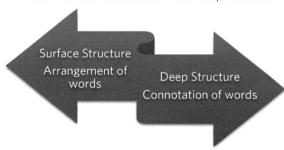

Chomsky also noted that the grammars of different languages are surprisingly similar. He believed that humans are born with a language acquisition device, which facilitates language acquisition when switched on by exposure to language during the critical period for language learning.

WORDS FOR SNOW

 It has been said that Eskimos have hundreds of words for snow. This claim may be an exaggeration, but it illustrates an important point: the number of words a culture has to describe something suggests the importance of that thing in that culture. Benjamin Whorf and Edward Sapir suggested the *theory of linguistic relativity* as an explanation for how language, to some extent, controls cognition. Can you think about something if you do not have words for it?

LANGUAGE ACQUISITION

FIRST WORDS

- **Cooing**

Infants use phonemes that do not resemble real words.

- **Babbling**

Next, infants use phonemes to convey meaning. Holophrases are single words conveying broader meanings.

Given their limited vocabularies, infants often overextend word meanings.

Even deaf infants babble.

Infants can pronounce phonemes from every language, but those that are not used are lost.

- **Telegraphic speech**

At around two years old, infants have developed a vocabulary of about 100 words.

They can combine a few words together to create simple commands, usually lacking parts of speech.

- **Overgeneralization**

Between two and three years of age, vocabulary expands exponentially.

Children learning the rules of grammar often overgeneralize and misapply the rules.

- **Adult speech**

By the age of 10, children have language abilities similar to those of an adult.

CREATIVITY AND PROBLEM SOLVING

STROKE OF GENIUS

Deductive reasoning: Drawing specific conclusions from general statements.

Inductive reasoning: Drawing general conclusions from specific observations.

Divergent thinking: Searching for several solutions.

Convergent thinking: Searching for a single answer.

Heuristic: Rule of thumb used to make a quick judgment.

Availability heuristic: Judgment based on whatever information comes to mind first.

Representativeness heuristic: Judgment based on comparison with a prototype.

Algorithm: Rule that determines guaranteed answers

Mental set: Rigid thought pattern.

Functional fixedness: Tendency to use objects only for their designed purpose.

Confirmation bias: Tendency to look for information that supports a preexisting viewpoint.

Hindsight bias: Tendency to think you knew the outcome of an event in advance.

Belief perseverance: Inability to accept contradictory evidence.

CRAM QUIZ
Language and Creativity

QUESTION 1

Which of the following elements of language is defined as the smallest meaningful unit of sound?

(A) phonemes
(B) morphemes
(C) syntax
(D) semantics
(E) pragmatics

QUESTION 2

Which of the following elements of language is defined as the use of language based on context?

(A) phonemes
(B) morphemes
(C) syntax
(D) semantics
(E) pragmatics

QUESTION 3

What theory of language acquisition is supported by Chomsky's language acquisition device?

(A) nativist theories
(B) emergentist theories
(C) social interactionist theories
(D) statistical learning theories
(E) relational frame theories

QUESTION 4

The idea that labeling objects influences cognition is known as the

(A) holophrastic theory
(B) naming diversification theory
(C) deep structure theory
(D) linguistic theory of relativity
(E) cognitive limitation theory

QUESTION 5

Which of the following statements is NOT an example of telegraphic speech?

(A) "Give cookie."
(B) "Want mommy."
(C) "Go potty now."
(D) "Doggy play ball."
(E) "I want dinner."

QUESTION 6

An infant sees a horse for the first time and shouts, "Doggy!" This is an example of

(A) overregularization
(B) overextension
(C) transformational grammar
(D) babbling
(E) chunking

QUESTION 7

You are given a box and asked to think of as many uses for it as possible in 60 seconds but have great difficulty coming up with many. What does your thought process exemplify?

(A) convergent thinking
(B) divergent thinking
(C) functional fixedness
(D) confirmation bias
(E) belief perseverance

QUESTION 8

During an election season, Geoff plans to vote for the Republican candidate. He chooses to watch and read only conservative news. What does this behavior exemplify?

(A) inductive reasoning
(B) mental set
(C) belief perseverance
(D) hindsight bias
(E) confirmation bias

ANSWERS

1. B
2. E
3. A
4. D
5. E
6. B
7. C
8. E

MOTIVATION AND EMOTION
Motivation

THEORIES OF MOTIVATION

WHAT YOU WANT AND WHAT YOU NEED

Motivations are the needs and desires that cause behaviors—the reasons people do the things they do. Intrinsic motivation comes from within oneself, while extrinsic motivation is drawn from the outside world.

DRIVE REDUCTION THEORY

- People are motivated by biological needs
- Drives are impulses to meet those needs in order to achieve homeostasis, a state of internal balance
- Primary drives are biological needs (food, shelter)
- Secondary drives are used to meet primary drives (money, acceptance)

INSTINCT THEORY

- People perform species-specific behaviors
- Instincts are inborn behaviors necessary for survival

INCENTIVE THEORY

- People perform some behaviors based on desire, rather than need
- Incentives are stimuli associated with rewards

OPPONENT PROCESS THEORY

- People begin at a baseline level of motivation
- Performing pleasurable behaviors moves people away from the baseline, but an opponent process motivates them to return to the neutral state
- This theory is often used to explain addiction: people use substances for pleasure but are then motivated to return to baseline; when they experience withdrawal, however, they often use the substance again to return to a neutral state

AROUSAL THEORY

- People try to achieve a balanced level of excitement
- The Yerkes-Dodson law states that people perform best at tasks that elicit medium levels of arousal

SOCIAL THEORY

- People respond to pressures from society
- Henry Murray classified 20 types of needs, such as needs for affiliation and for cognitive dissonance
- Kurt Lewin named 4 types of motivational conflict: approach-approach (two pleasant choices), avoidance-avoidance (two unpleasant choices), approach-avoidance (one choice with pros and cons), and multiple approach-avoidance (many choices with pros and cons)

HIERARCHY OF NEEDS

CLIMBING THE PYRAMID

Abraham Maslow created a hierarchy of needs, predicting the order in which needs must be satisfied.

HUNGER AND EATING DISORDERS

THROUGH THICK AND THIN

Hunger is determined by an empty stomach and body chemistry (glucose and insulin). The *hypothalamus* helps stimulate and satiate hunger. *Set-point theory* states that the hypothalamus maintains the body's optimum body weight by determining the metabolic rate. Eating disorders are psychological problems related to weight, body image, and eating habits.

SEX

THE BIRDS AND THE BEES

Humans are driven to procreate in order to pass on their genes. The hypothalamus stimulates the pituitary gland to produce sexual hormones (androgens and estrogens). Researchers of human sexuality include Alfred Kinsey, William Masters, and Virginia Johnson.

SEXUAL RESPONSE CYCLE

Excitement
Heart and respiration rates increase; penis and clitoris swell

Plateau
Heart and respiration rates remain elevated; muscle tension increases; genitals secrete fluids

Orgasm
Heart and respiration rates increase further; genitals contract; males ejaculate

Resolution
Heart and respiration rates decrease; muscles relax; men have a refractory period in which they cannot have another orgasm

CRAM QUIZ
Motivation

QUESTION 1

Which of the following is an example of a secondary drive?

(A) food
(B) thirst
(C) shelter
(D) acceptance
(E) sex

QUESTION 2

Jackson drank a few beers in order to loosen up at a party but wants to return to his normal state later in the evening. He feels hungover, however, and decides to drink more beer in attempt to feel better. What theory of motivation does this behavior exemplify?

(A) drive reduction theory
(B) instinct theory
(C) opponent process theory
(D) arousal theory
(E) incentive theory

QUESTION 3

Which of the following is NOT one of Lewin's categories of motivational conflict?

(A) approach-approach
(B) avoidance-avoidance
(C) approach-avoidance
(D) multiple approach-avoidance
(E) binding approach-avoidance

QUESTION 4

What need is at the top of Maslow's hierarchy?

(A) self-actualization
(B) belongingness
(C) self-esteem
(D) survival
(E) safety

QUESTION 5

According to the lipostatic hypothesis, what substance is used to monitor the amount of fat in the body?

(A) glucose
(B) leptin
(C) insulin
(D) androgens
(E) cortisol

QUESTION 6

Lesions in the lateral hypothalamus are most likely to result in

(A) excessive eating
(B) decreased drinking
(C) excessive sexual desire
(D) increased exercise
(E) decreased sleep

QUESTION 7

During which phase of the sexual response cycle does the penis become erect?

(A) initial excitement
(B) plateau
(C) orgasm
(D) resolution
(E) refractory period

QUESTION 8

During which phase of the sexual response cycle do genital contractions occur?

(A) initial excitement
(B) plateau
(C) orgasm
(D) resolution
(E) refractory period

ANSWERS

1. D
2. C
3. E
4. A
5. B
6. B
7. A
8. C

MOTIVATION AND EMOTION
Emotion

THEORIES OF EMOTION

THE CHICKEN OR THE EGG?

Emotions are thoughts and feelings that occur in response to external stimuli. These are accompanied by physiological arousal, but psychologists debate whether the physiological change occurs before or after the emotional response.

Influences on Emotion

James-Lange Theory

- Emotion is caused by physiological change
- Frightening stimulus appears ↓ Heart races ↓ Feel afraid
- Theory is problematic because certain physiological states are common to several emotional states

Cannon-Bard Theory

- Physiological changes and emotional experiences occur at the same time
- Frightening stimulus appears ↓ Heart races and feel afraid
- Theory involves biology and cognition

Two-Factor (Schacter-Singer) Theory

- Physiological changes occur, followed by cognitive labeling of the emotional state
- Frightening stimulus appears ↓ Heart races ↓ Recognize that something scary happened ↓ Feel afraid
- People in an aroused physiological state experience more intense emotional states

STRESS

STRESS CAUSES *GAS*

Life is full of stressors that make people feel challenged and threatened. Some stressors are transient, while others are chronic. Hans Selye developed the concept of the general adaptation syndrome (GAS) to describe responses to stressors.

Alarm ➡
- Sympathetic nervous system is aroused
- The body prepares itself to meet challenge

Resistance ➡
- Parasympathetic nervous system begins to reduce arousal
- The body releases hormones to maintain its ability to deal with stressor, but resources will be used up if stressor persists

Exhaustion
- Parasympathetic nervous system returns to normal
- Resources are depleted
- The immune system is compromised

According to Richard Lazarus, people cognitively evaluate stressors. The primary appraisal involves determining whether an occurrence is stressful. The secondary appraisal involves determining one's ability to handle the occurrence if it is stressful. The stress worsens if the individual is incapable of handling the stressor and decreases if the individual is able to handle the stressor.

TYPE A AND TYPE B PERSONALITIES

THE ABC'S OF STRESS RESPONSE

Individuals respond to stress in different ways, but the main response patterns have been split into two categories: Type-A and Type-B.

TYPE-A PERSONALITY
- Aggressive and urgent response to stressors
- Competitive
- Seeks out demanding activities
- May be more susceptible to stress-induced illness

TYPE-B PERSONALITY
- Requires more to get stressed
- When stressed, usually not to the same extent as Type-A personalities
- Easy-going

CRAM QUIZ
Emotion

QUESTION 1

Maya feels her heart race and her palms sweat as she simultaneously recognizes that she is nervous. What theory of emotion does this exemplify?

(A) James-Lange theory
(B) Cannon-Bard theory
(C) two-factor theory
(D) Schacter-Singer theory
(E) general adaptation theory

QUESTION 2

According to the two-factor theory, which of the following people would likely experience the most intense emotions?

(A) a sprinter
(B) a television watcher
(C) a writer
(D) an artist
(E) a walker

QUESTION 3

Who developed the concept of the general adaptation syndrome?

(A) Lazarus
(B) Lange
(C) Bard
(D) Singer
(E) Selye

QUESTION 4

People with Type-B personalities can best be described as

(A) competitive
(B) rushed
(C) aggressive
(D) easy-going
(E) reactive

QUESTION 5

Why does stress impair the immune system?

(A) The body becomes overwhelmed with excess hormones released in response to the stress.
(B) The body forces itself to rest in order to recover from persistent arousal.
(C) The body's resources are depleted by arousal.
(D) The body cannot return its heart and respiration rates to normal after extended arousal.
(E) The body experiences a state of shock after dealing with the stressor.

QUESTION 6

Who divided the stress response into primary and secondary appraisals?

(A) Lazarus
(B) Lange
(C) Bard
(D) Singer
(E) Selye

QUESTION 7

According to the Cannon-Bard theory, which part of the brain sends information to the autonomic nervous system?

(A) amygdala
(B) temporal lobe
(C) pons
(D) cerebellum
(E) thalamus

QUESTION 8

Holmes and Rahe's social readjustment rating scale measures stress according to

(A) cortisol secretion levels
(B) heart rates
(C) life change units
(D) emotional reaction appraisals
(E) physiological arousal increments

ANSWERS

1. B
2. A
3. E
4. D
5. C
6. A
7. E
8. C

SOCIAL PSYCHOLOGY
Group Dynamics, Attribution, and Interpersonal Perception

GROUPS

US AND THEM

Social psychology is the study of how people interact with each other. Some interaction occurs one on one, while some takes place in groups.

Social faciliation

- Improved performance of well-learned tasks in the presence of others

Social loafing

- Tendency to exert less effort on a group task than if one were working alone

Group polarization

- Strengthening of the dominant opinion in a group through the course of discussion

Deindividuation

- Abandonment of self-awareness as an anonymous member of a group

Groupthink

- Members of a group agree in order to preserve group harmony

ATTRIBUTION THEORY

TAKING THE BLAME

People tend to explain their own behaviors and those of others in predictable ways. **Attribution** is the placement of responsibility for behaviors on internal disposition or external situations.

The **fundamental attribution error** is the tendency to infer that others' actions reflect their dispositions more so than their situations. Alternatively, people tend to explain negative occurrences in their lives based on situational factors rather than internal causes, while successes are attributed to oneself; this tendency is known as the **self-serving bias**.

According to the **just-world bias**, good things happen to good people and bad things happen to bad people. Most people would like to believe that victims deserve whatever happened to them and that they themselves can avoid misfortune by being a good person.

Sometimes, making attributions can impact future behaviors. When one person expects another to achieve or fail, that person is likely to fulfill those expectations. This is known as a **self-fulfilling prophecy**.

People often overestimate the number of other people who share their views. This is known as the **false-consensus effect**.

INTERPERSONAL PERCEPTION

GETTING TO KNOW ALL ABOUT YOU

Interpersonal attraction is based on a variety of factors, from physical appearance to background. People find out about each other through self-disclosure, the process of sharing personal details. Mutual liking, frequent contact, and similar interests further the attraction.

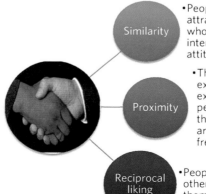

Similarity
- People are attracted to others who have similar interests and attitudes

Proximity
- The mere exposure effect explains how people tend to like those whom they are around frequently

Reciprocal liking
- People usually like others who like them

CRAM QUIZ
Group Dynamics, Attribution, and Interpersonal Perception

QUESTION 1

A cyclist performs better during a race with others than when she races against the clock by herself. This is best explained by

(A) social facilitation
(B) social loafing
(C) deindividuation
(D) self-fulfilling prophecies
(E) self-serving biases

QUESTION 2

Joe is working on a group project and finds himself doing all the work while the other members of his group slack off. Which theory of group dynamics does this behavior exemplify?

(A) social facilitation
(B) social loafing
(C) deindividuation
(D) social inhibition
(E) group polarization

QUESTION 3

Before attending a meeting, Tony says that he is vehemently against his employer's new budget plan. At the meeting, though, everybody else seems content with the plan. Tony does not want to cause any problems, so he agrees with the budget. What theory of group dynamics does this behavior exemplify?

(A) social loafing
(B) false-consensus effect
(C) deindividuation
(D) social inhibition
(E) groupthink

QUESTION 4

People often misjudge the extent to which others agree with their ideas. This is known as the

(A) self-serving bias
(B) fundamental attribution error
(C) false-consensus effect
(D) just-world bias
(E) self-fulfilling prophecy

QUESTION 5

The tendency to blame other peoples' behaviors on their internal dispositions is known as the

(A) self-serving bias
(B) fundamental attribution error
(C) false-consensus effect
(D) just-world bias
(E) self-fulfilling prophecy

QUESTION 6

The tendency to believe that a person with one positive trait has other positive traits is known as the

(A) just-world bias
(B) fundamental attribution error
(C) mere exposure effect
(D) halo effect
(E) reciprocal liking effect

QUESTION 7

Jennifer begins a new job and is somewhat attracted to her colleague in the cubicle next to her. She sees him every day, and her attraction increases. This can most likely be attributed to

(A) the mere exposure effect
(B) the halo effect
(C) similarity
(D) physical attractiveness
(E) reciprocal liking

QUESTION 8

Which of the following researchers coined the term "groupthink"?

(A) Latane
(B) Darley
(C) Bandura
(D) Sherif
(E) Janis

ANSWERS

1. A
2. B
3. E
4. C
5. B
6. D
7. A
8. E

SOCIAL PSYCHOLOGY
Attitudes and Antisocial/Prosocial Behavior

ATTITUDES AND PERSUASION

GETTING AN ATTITUDE ADJUSTMENT

Attitudes are thoughts and feelings about stimuli such as people, places, and events. They are conditioned to be positive or negative based on prior experiences. Attitudes can be changed through persuasion.

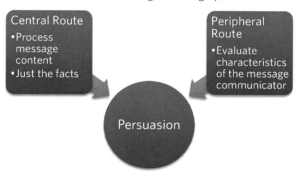

Central Route
- Process message content
- Just the facts

Peripheral Route
- Evaluate characteristics of the message communicator

Persuasion

Features of the *message* that may increase persuasiveness:
- Frequent repetition
- Fear-inducing
- For an uninformed audience, a single-sided message
- For an informed audience, acknowledgement of opposing arguments

Features of the *communicator* that may increase persuasiveness:
- Attractive
- Famous
- Knowledgeable
- Likeable
- Trustworthy

Features of an easily persuaded *audience*:
- Low self-esteem
- Low educational level

COGNITIVE DISSONANCE

Cognitive dissonance results from a conflict between attitudes and behaviors. People typically change one or the other in order to achieve consistency and relieve tension. *Leon Festinger* found that people are more likely to change their attitudes to match their behaviors than vice versa.

AGGRESSION AND ANTISOCIAL BEHAVIOR

HATE ME TODAY, HATE ME TOMORROW

Aggression is behavior intended to hurt someone.

Instrumental aggression is used to gain or achieve something

Hostile aggression is usually impulsive, emotional, and lacking a clear purpose

The frustration-aggression hypothesis suggests that people who feel frustrated are more likely to behave aggressively. Aggression may also be an adaptive response, or it may result from observing aggressive models.

ALTRUISM AND PROSOCIAL BEHAVIOR

HELP! I NEED SOMEBODY

Altruism is a selfless sacrifice—help given without personal gain.

Bystander intervention is the influence of nearby people on the likelihood of helping. This was exemplified in the case of Kitty Genovese, a New Yorker who was stabbed to death outside her apartment complex while neighbors heard her scream. No one helped her because each person assumed that somebody else was already helping. This phenomenon is called *diffusion of responsibility*: the more people around when help is needed, the less each person feels responsible to help.

STEREOTYPES, PREJUDICE, DISCRIMINATION

REBEL WITHOUT A CAUSE

Stereotypes
- Prototypes of people based on common attributes of group members
- Useful for quick categorization but harmful when assumptions are false

Prejudice
- Pre-judging of groups of people
- Negative attitude exists without evidence
- Can result from overapplication of stereotypes

Discrimination
- Acting on prejudice by treating members of a stereotyped group differently
- Prejudice = attitude; discrimination = behavior

CRAM QUIZ
Attitudes and Antisocial/Prosocial Behavior

QUESTION 1

Which of the following individuals would likely be easiest to persuade?

- (A) a graduate student with low self-esteem
- (B) a doctor with high self-esteem
- (C) a high school dropout with low self-esteem
- (D) a college student with low self-esteem
- (E) a high school graduate with high self-esteem

QUESTION 2

Leon Festinger asked subjects to perform a boring task and tell other subjects the task was enjoyable. Participants were paid either $1 or $20 for lying. Those with less motivation to lie were more likely to say they actually enjoyed the task. What caused this reaction?

- (A) cognitive dissonance
- (B) peripheral persuasion
- (C) bystander intervention
- (D) foot-in-the-door phenomenon
- (E) pluralistic ignorance

QUESTION 3

An old lady drops a bag of groceries while carrying them to her car. Though there are many people around, nobody offers to help. This is likely the result of

- (A) dehumanization
- (B) altruism
- (C) prejudice
- (D) diffusion of responsibility
- (E) social loafing

QUESTION 4

Which of the following is NOT an example of instrumental aggression?

- (A) Katie pushes Mindy out of line so she can get lunch first.
- (B) Roy punches Eric when Eric calls him a bad name.
- (C) Mike shoves Jeri so he can steal her toy.
- (D) Russ hits Phil's car in order to get to a parking space first.
- (E) Brian mugs Ed in order to steal his wallet.

QUESTION 5

Unfriendly Inn refuses to serve Asian customers. This policy is an example of

- (A) stereotyping
- (B) prejudice
- (C) discrimination
- (D) aggression
- (E) prosocial behavior

QUESTION 6

According to the contact hypothesis, people are most likely to reduce stereotypes if they

- (A) list positive attributes of members of other groups
- (B) trade places with members of other groups
- (C) work toward a common goal with members of other groups
- (D) physically fight members of other groups
- (E) spend time with members of other groups

QUESTION 7

A fire alarm goes off in a classroom. All the students look around at each other, see that nobody else is moving, and decide to stay seated. This behavior is an example of

- (A) pluralistic ignorance
- (B) cognitive dissonance
- (C) diffusion of responsibility
- (D) bystander intervention
- (E) peripheral persuasion

QUESTION 8

An advertisement does not provide information about a product, instead trying to sell it through attractive models and flashy graphics. What does this ad exemplify?

- (A) door-in-the-face phenomenon
- (B) peripheral persuasion
- (C) cognitive dissonance
- (D) central persuasion
- (E) pluralistic ignorance

ANSWERS

1. C
2. A
3. D
4. B
5. C
6. E
7. A
8. B

SOCIAL PSYCHOLOGY
Conformity, Compliance, and Obedience

OBEDIENCE

SHOCKING DEMANDS

"We will pay you $4.00 for 1 hour of your time. Persons needed for a study of memory."
– Milgram's advertisement for participants

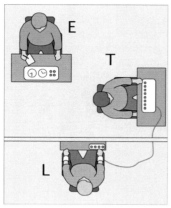

http://en.wikipedia.org/wiki/File:Milgram_Experiment_v2.png

Stanley Milgram recruited approximately 500 people to participate in a study of obedience at Yale University in 1974. The experimenter (E, in illustration above) told the teacher (T, the research participant), to give electric shocks to a learner (L) when the learner performed poorly on a task. The participant believed that the learner was receiving actual shocks, though the learner was really a confederate who played pre-recorded screaming sounds. The experimenter instructed the teacher to continue giving increasingly painful shocks, despite the protests of the learner. The majority of participants obeyed the experimenter.

The more authority the participant believed the experimenter had, the more likely the participant was to continue shocking the learner—participants were thus more likely to continue if they thought the experimenter was a professor, rather than a graduate student. When participants saw other confederates refuse to continue the shocks, however, the participant was less likely to continue shocking the learner. Obedience to the experimenter's instructions also decreased when the participant could see the learners, rather than only hearing them.

This experiment provides extremely interesting information about the nature of obedience, though it would likely never be permitted by an Institutional Review Board (IRB) today. Research participants were later told that the shocks were faked, but the realization that participants could have killed the learner had the situation been real was naturally quite disturbing to those involved.

COMPLIANCE

DEATH OF A SALESMAN

Compliance is acting on someone else's request, even if it goes against your own self-interest.

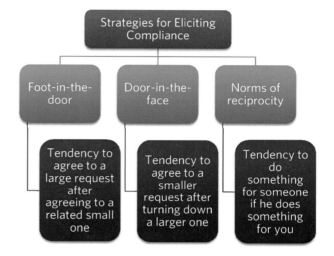

CONFORMITY

ONE AND THE SAME

If you have ever been to middle school (or high school, for that matter), you probably know a great deal about conformity. **Conformity** is a change in one's behavior in order to match other group members. Groups of three or more members can elicit changes in behavior, particularly when members appear to be cohesive and unanimous in their opinions.

SOLOMON ASCH

- Asch asked participants to take part in a study about perceptual judgment
- Participants were put into groups of confederates and asked to match the lengths of two lines in different groups (see illustration at right)

http://en.wikipedia.org/wiki/File:Asch_experiment.png

- Group members answered one at a time
- The answer should have been obvious, but confederates purposely answered incorrectly
- Participants usually agreed with group members, even though they knew the answer was wrong

CRAM QUIZ
Conformity, Compliance, and Obedience

QUESTION 1

Which of the following factors was NOT correlated with likelihood of conforming to a group in Asch's conformity experiments?

(A) gender
(B) age
(C) social status
(D) group cohesiveness
(E) group unanimity

QUESTION 2

A girl scout tries to sell a box of cookies for $10 but is turned down. She then offers the box for $5 and successfully sells the cookies. This is an example of the

(A) door-in-the-face approach
(B) foot-in-the-door approach
(C) norms of reciprocity
(D) bargaining approach
(E) norms of social influence

QUESTION 3

Stanley Milgram's electric shock experiment studied

(A) aggression
(B) compliance
(C) discrimination
(D) obedience
(E) conformity

QUESTION 4

In Solomon Asch's conformity experiments, participants were asked to make judgments about

(A) moral values
(B) fashion choices
(C) perceptual pairings
(D) accuracy of trivia knowledge
(E) pain level thresholds

QUESTION 5

A wildlife foundation sends you an adorable plush dolphin for free, along with a letter requesting a donation. You decide to send them $10 since the foundation gave you a free gift. This is an example of the

(A) door-in-the-face approach
(B) foot-in-the-door approach
(C) norms of reciprocity
(D) bargaining approach
(E) norms of social influence

QUESTION 6

A false participant used by a researcher to elicit responses from actual research participants is known as a(n)

(A) learner
(B) modeler
(C) persuader
(D) faker
(E) confederate

QUESTION 7

How many people (other than the participant) are needed in order for conformity to occur?

(A) two
(B) three
(C) four
(D) five
(E) six

QUESTION 8

People are most likely to obey someone who is

(A) friendly
(B) attractive
(C) rude
(D) authoritative
(E) intelligent

ANSWERS

1. B
2. A
3. D
4. C
5. C
6. E
7. B
8. D

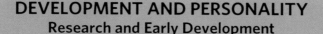

DEVELOPMENT AND PERSONALITY
Research and Early Development

PRENATAL DEVELOPMENT AND THE NEWBORN

A REFLEXIVE BUNDLE OF JOY

Prenatal development occurs in stages from conception to birth.

Zygote
- Fertilized egg
- Cells divide
- Implants into uterine wall

Embryo
- Organs form
- Lasts from 2 weeks to about 2 or 3 months

Fetus
- Rapid growth
- Sexual differentiation
- Moves in response to sound

During the prenatal stage, babies are susceptible to harmful chemicals and viruses known as *teratogens*. Teratogens can pass through the placenta and cause birth defects; they include drugs, radiation, pollutants, and alcohol. Mothers who drink during pregnancy may cause *fetal alcohol syndrome*, which results in mental retardation and physical malformation.

REFLEXES

Humans have a variety of innate reflexes throughout life, but some reflexes are specific to newborns and disappear within the first few months of life.

Rooting reflex	Touching the baby's cheek causes him to turn his head to the side that was touched
Sucking reflex	Placing an object in a baby's mouth will cause him to suck on it
Grasping reflex	Placing an object into a baby's palm or the pad of his foot will cause the baby to try to grasp with his fingers or toes
Moro reflex	Startling will cause the baby to fling his limbs out and then retract them in order to appear small
Babinski reflex	Stroking the bottom of a baby's foot will cause him to splay his toes

RESEARCH AND DEVELOPMENTAL ISSUES

WOMB TO TOMB

Developmental psychology covers the entire human lifespan. Development occurs from conception to death—it does not end with adolescence. Some psychologists believe that it is *continuous*, or gradual, while others think it is *discontinuous*, meaning that it occurs in stages.

Developmental psychologists use two types of studies:

Cross-sectional research	• Compare people from different age groups over a short period of time to determine the effects of age on development • Fast and stable method
Longitudinal research	• Compare the same group of people over a long period of time to determine how they change • Slow and sometimes unstable method

ATTACHMENT AND PARENTING

MOMMY AND ME

Harry Harlow raised infant monkeys with either a soft terry cloth mother or a wire mother with a bottle. The monkeys preferred the comfort of the soft mother.

Mary Ainsworth researched human attachment by studying infants' behaviors in strange situations. Mothers briefly left infants alone in an unfamiliar room. Ainsworth observed three types of attachment:

1. **Secure**: confident when parent is present; distressed when parent leaves; seek comfort from parent upon return; 66% of participants
2. **Avoidant**: resist being held; explore the novel environment; do not seek comfort when parent returns; 21% of participants
3. **Resistant**: show ambivalence toward parent; distressed when parent leaves; resist comfort when parent returns; 12% of participants

Parents typically follow one of three parenting styles. Correlational research shows that the authoritative style produces the best results.

1. **Permissive**: no clear or consistent rules; minimal use of punishment; open to children's wishes
2. **Authoritative**: reasonable, consistent rules; rationales for rules are explained and discussed; balance of praise and punishment
3. **Authoritarian**: strict rules with expectation of obedience; rationales not provided; punish more than praise

CRAM QUIZ
Research and Early Development

QUESTION 1

What is the first stage of prenatal development?

(A) zygote
(B) fetus
(C) neonate
(D) embryo
(E) germinal

QUESTION 2

Harmful chemicals and viruses that negatively impact prenatal development are known as

(A) agents
(B) pollutants
(C) fetal effects
(D) teratogens
(E) drugs

QUESTION 3

A newborn baby hears a startling noise and responds by throwing out his arms and legs, as if to grab onto something. What reflex is this baby demonstrating?

(A) grasping reflex
(B) Moro reflex
(C) sucking reflex
(D) Babinski reflex
(E) rooting reflex

QUESTION 4

What reflex causes babies to splay their toes outward when the bottoms of their feet are stroked?

(A) grasping reflex
(B) Moro reflex
(C) sucking reflex
(D) Babinski reflex
(E) rooting reflex

QUESTION 5

Which of the following types of research follows the same group of people over an extended period of time?

(A) naturalistic observation
(B) case study
(C) longitudinal
(D) experimental
(E) cross-sectional

QUESTION 6

According to Harry Harlow's monkey research, which of the following characteristics of the mother monkey was most comforting to the infants?

(A) food attachment
(B) grooming capability
(C) vocalization
(D) defensive abilities
(E) physical comfort

QUESTION 7

In Mary Ainsworth's strange situation study, what attachment style was most common?

(A) secure
(B) avoidant
(C) ambivalent
(D) resistant
(E) anxious

QUESTION 8

According to correlational research, what parenting style produces the most socially capable children?

(A) permissive
(B) authoritative
(C) authoritarian
(D) ambivalent
(E) avoidant

ANSWERS

1. A
2. D
3. B
4. D
5. C
6. E
7. A
8. B

DEVELOPMENT AND PERSONALITY
Theories of Development

JEAN PIAGET

AGES AND STAGES OF COGNITIVE DEVELOPMENT

Piaget created a stage theory of cognitive development. He believed that all children gain skills in a fixed order by *assimilating* new information into existing categories and modifying categories to include new information through *accommodation*.

Sensorimotor

- Age: birth to 2 years
- Explore the world through the senses
- Develop object permanence
- Learn to coordinate motor activities to produce desired effects

Preoperational

- Age: 2 to 7
- Develop symbolic thinking and language skills
- Thought is egocentric

Concrete Operational

- Age: 7 to 12
- Develop understanding that the volume, area, and number of an object stay the same even when the object is moved or rearranged (conservation)

Formal Operational

- Age: 12 to adulthood
- Develop abstract thinking abilities
- Capable of thinking about one's own cognitive abilities (metacognition)

CRITICISMS OF PIAGETIAN THEORY

- Based on case studies of his own children
- Underestimates children's abilities
- Lacks recognition of environmental influences
- Overemphasizes language abilities
- Overly discontinuous
- Stages progress too slowly

SIGMUND FREUD

PSYCHOSEXUAL STAGES

Freud believed that development proceeds through psychosexual stages based on erogenous zones. Failure to move through the stages results in fixation.

Stage	Pleasure Center	Fixation
Oral	Mouth	Overeating, smoking; dependency
Anal	Anus	Overly controlling (anal retentive) or out of control
Phallic	Genitals	Relationship problems (based on resolution of Oedipus or Electra complexes)
Genital	Genitals	After passing through a latency period, fixation is normal for sexual pleasure

LEV VYGOTSKY

IN THE ZONE

Vygotsky believed that knowledge develops by internalizing information from socialization. He suggested that children have a *zone of proximal development*, a range between what they can do with and without help.

ERIK ERIKSON

NEVER-ENDING CRISES

In Erikson's stages of psychosocial development, individuals must pass through a series of crises.

TRUST VS. MISTRUST
Age 0-1: Determine whether needs can be met

AUTONOMY VS. SHAME AND DOUBT
Age 1-3: Develop control over body and environment

INITIATIVE VS. GUILT
Age 3-6: Learn to balance assertiveness

INDUSTRY VS. INFERIORITY
Age 6-12: Develop sense of accomplishment

IDENTITY VS. ROLE CONFUSION
Adolescence: Develop personal values

INTIMACY VS. ISOLATION
Early adulthood: Form meaningful relationships

GENERATIVITY VS. STAGNATION
Middle adulthood: Try to make a difference in the world

INTEGRITY VS. DESPAIR
Old age: Evaluate personal successes and failures

CRAM QUIZ
Theories of Development

QUESTION 1

Which of the following develops during Piaget's sensorimotor stage?

(A) symbolic thinking
(B) language skills
(C) object permanence
(D) understanding of conservation
(E) abstract thought

QUESTION 2

Jacob pours one cup of water from a short, fat glass to a tall, skinny glass. When asked how much water he has after pouring, he understands that the volume is the same as it was before. When is this skill developed?

(A) sensorimotor stage
(B) preoperational stage
(C) operational stage
(D) concrete operational stage
(E) formal operational stage

QUESTION 3

What type of research did Piaget perform when creating his theory of cognitive development?

(A) case study
(B) experiment
(C) survey
(D) cross-sectional
(E) correlational

QUESTION 4

In which of Freud's psychosexual stages does the Oedipus complex occur?

(A) oral
(B) anal
(C) phallic
(D) latency
(E) genital

QUESTION 5

Evan is a neat freak who must have everything perfectly organized and in its place. According to Freud's psychosexual theory, in what stage of development is Evan fixated?

(A) oral
(B) anal
(C) phallic
(D) latency
(E) genital

QUESTION 6

Who developed the theory of a zone of proximal development?

(A) Kohlberg
(B) Piaget
(C) Erikson
(D) Freud
(E) Vygotsky

QUESTION 7

Which of Erikson's psychosocial stages occurs at the end of the lifespan?

(A) integrity vs. despair
(B) intimacy vs. role confusion
(C) autonomy vs. shame and doubt
(D) generativity vs. stagnation
(E) industry vs. inferiority

QUESTION 8

Which of Erikson's psychosocial stages focuses on leaving a mark on the world?

(A) integrity vs. despair
(B) identity vs. role confusion
(C) trust vs. mistrust
(D) generativity vs. stagnation
(E) autonomy vs. shame and doubt

ANSWERS

1. C
2. D
3. A
4. C
5. B
6. E
7. A
8. D

DEVELOPMENT AND PERSONALITY
Moral and Gender Development

MORAL DEVELOPMENT

TWO WRONGS DON'T MAKE A RIGHT

Lawrence Kohlberg devised a three-stage theory of morality development.

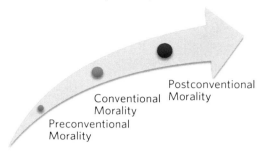

Postconventional Morality

Conventional Morality

Preconventional Morality

Preconventional Morality

Below age 9	Avoid punishment; earn rewards	Moral choices based on self-interest

Conventional Morality

Age 9 through adolescence	Internalize societal rules	Moral decisions based on law and convention

Postconventional Morality

Adolescence and adulthood	Moral decisions based on personal values of what is right, fair, and ethical, even if that defies law and social rules	Few people reach this level

Carol Gilligan criticized Kohlberg's theory, arguing that it is based primarily on research of boys. She said that girls and boys develop morality differently, with boys making more absolute decisions and girls judging situational factors. Other researchers have argued that Kohlberg's theory does not adequately describe non-Western cultures.

GENDER DEVELOPMENT

WHAT ARE LITTLE GIRLS AND BOYS MADE OF?

- *Gender identity*: children are aware of their gender and able to label themselves as boys or girls by the age of two or three
- *Gender typing*: children usually fulfill sex-related roles between the ages of two and seven
- *Gender constancy*: children realize that gender is a fixed individual characteristic between the ages of two and seven

LEARNING GENDER

Albert Bandura believed that gender roles are developed through social learning: young children see older children being rewarded for fulfilling their gender roles and punished for stepping outside them. The younger children then aim to behave as expected, creating a modeling cycle for future generations.

Research does show that parents typically reward boys for behaving independently and competitively and engaging in rough play while girls are rewarded for being nurturing, caring, and dependent.

According to Freud, gender development occurs through competition: boys compete with their fathers for their mothers' attention. This competition is known as the *Oedipus complex*, named after the Greek tragedy in which Oedipus kills his father and marries his mother. Boys eventually realize that if they cannot beat their fathers, they might as well join them, and they come to identify with males.

Similarly, girls compete with their mothers for their fathers' attention. This is, after all, why some are called "daddy's girls." Freud called this phenomenon the *Electra complex* after another Greek character who wants to avenge her father's death by killing her mother. Girls also learn to identify with their mothers and internalize female gender roles.

Freud's psychosexual theories have not been supported empirically.

CRAM QUIZ
Moral and Gender Development

QUESTION 1

Six-year-old Evan says he does not want to misbehave because his parents will give him a time out. What type of morality is he following?

(A) preconventional
(B) conventional
(C) postconventional
(D) concrete operational
(E) formal operational

QUESTION 2

Isabelle believes that there are principles of universal justice that supersede legal rules of right and wrong. What type of morality does she follow?

(A) preconventional
(B) conventional
(C) postconventional
(D) concrete operational
(E) formal operational

QUESTION 3

Carol Gilligan criticized Kohlberg's theory of morality development because she believed that it did not apply to

(A) minorities
(B) older adults
(C) men
(D) women
(E) religious individuals

QUESTION 4

The concept of gender as a fixed characteristic is known as

(A) gender identity
(B) gender constancy
(C) gender typing
(D) gender modeling
(E) gender roles

QUESTION 5

What psychological theory suggests that gender roles develop from modeling and imitation?

(A) behaviorist
(B) humanistic
(C) psychodynamic
(D) biopsychological
(E) vicarious learning

QUESTION 6

Freud's theory that young girls compete with their mothers for their fathers' attention is known as the

(A) Oedipus complex
(B) Clytemnestra complex
(C) Agamemnon complex
(D) Electra complex
(E) Antigone complex

QUESTION 7

According to Kohlberg, a 13-year-old is most likely to base moral decisions on

(A) law and social convention
(B) personal beliefs about right and wrong
(C) avoidance of punishment
(D) desire for rewards
(E) universal principles of justice

QUESTION 8

By what age do children typically establish gender identity?

(A) three
(B) five
(C) seven
(D) eleven
(E) thirteen

ANSWERS

1. A
2. C
3. D
4. B
5. E
6. D
7. A
8. A

DEVELOPMENT AND PERSONALITY
Theories of Personality

PSYCHOANALYTIC AND PSYCHODYNAMIC

DELVING INTO THE UNCONSCIOUS

Freud developed his psychoanalytic theory of personality based on his belief in the division of the conscious and unconscious mind. Followers of Freud combined his ideas with more modern concepts to create psychodynamic theory.

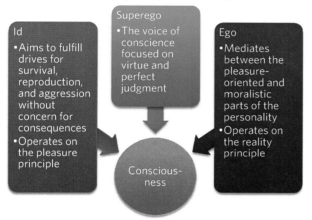

Conflict between the id and ego creates anxiety, which people reduce through defense mechanisms.

- **Repression**: Remove unpleasant thoughts from the conscious mind
- **Regression**: Return to comforting, childish behaviors
- **Reaction formation**: Convert unacceptable impulses into their opposites
- **Projection**: Attributes one's own threatening impulses to someone else
- **Rationalization**: Justify behavior to make it unthreatening
- **Displacement**: Redirect unacceptable or dangerous impulses toward acceptable or safe ones

Psychodynamic Theorists

Karen Horney	Questioned male bias of Freud's work; developed theory of personality based on one's need for security
Carl Jung	Believed that people have personal unconsciousness, which contains repressed memories, and collective unconsciousness, which comprises universal concepts called archetypes
Alfred Adler	Thought that people develop feelings of inferiority, which can be overcome by contributing to society

HUMANISTIC THEORIES

THE BRIGHT SIDE OF LIFE

The humanistic approach to personality is holistic and views people as innately good and capable of free will.

Carl Rogers believed that people have **self-concepts**, which are mental representations of themselves. Further, Rogers argued that placing **conditions of worth** on others harms one's self-concept. He felt that all people should be treated with **unconditional positive regard**, meaning that they should be valued regardless of their successes or failures.

Carl Rogers and Abraham Maslow both believed that people are capable of **self-actualization**, which is the fulfillment of an individual's potential.

SOCIAL-COGNITIVE THEORIES

TAKING CONTROL

These theories of personality assume that personality is based on cognitive constructs.

Albert Bandura	Julian Rotter	George Kelly
Personality is influenced by self-efficacy, which is a person's perception of his own abilities	Internal locus of control: believe successes and failures result from individual efforts	Behavior is influenced by cognition
If you believe you can accomplish something, you are more likely to actually succeed	External locus of control: believe successes and failures result from chance	Future behavior can be predicted based on past behavior
		People evaluate the world using personal constructs

TRAIT THEORIES

THE BIG FIVE

- **Traits** are stable characteristics that predispose individuals to behave in a particular way
- Trait theorists generally agree that traits are inherited but disagree about how to categorize traits
- **Nomothetic** traits are universal sets of traits; **idiographic** traits describe an individual
- The Big Five personality traits: Openness, Conscientiousness, Extroversion, Agreeableness, Neuroticism (OCEAN)
- **Gordon Allport** created a hierarchy of trait types: cardinal traits, primary traits, and secondary traits
- **Raymond Cattell** believed that all people have varying degrees of 16 basic traits
- **Hans Eysenck** classified individuals along a scale of introversion-extraversion and stable-unstable
- **Walter Mischel** argued that traits vary based on one's circumstances

CRAM QUIZ
Theories of Personality

QUESTION 1

Dean is angry at his boss at work, so he goes home and yells at his wife and kicks his dog. What defense mechanism does this behavior exemplify?

(A) regression
(B) reaction formation
(C) projection
(D) rationalization
(E) displacement

QUESTION 2

According to psychoanalytic theory, which part of the personality operates on the pleasure principle?

(A) id
(B) ego
(C) superego
(D) collective unconscious
(E) archetype

QUESTION 3

Which psychodynamic theorist believed that personality is a product of birth order and feelings of inferiority?

(A) Horney
(B) Jung
(C) Adler
(D) Klein
(E) Freud

QUESTION 4

Which psychodynamic theorist believed that all people have an anima and animus (feminine and masculine) side to their personalities?

(A) Horney
(B) Jung
(C) Adler
(D) Klein
(E) Freud

QUESTION 5

Toby fails his algebra test and goes home worried that his parents will be upset with him. When his mother tells him that she loves no matter how he performs at school, what humanistic principle is she demonstrating?

(A) self-actualization
(B) determinism
(C) incongruence
(D) unconditional positive regard
(E) conditions of worth

QUESTION 6

Which of the following psychologists posits that personality is influenced by locus of control?

(A) Bandura
(B) Allport
(C) Cattell
(D) Kelly
(E) Rotter

QUESTION 7

Which of the following is not one of the Big Five personality traits?

(A) Openness
(B) Agreeableness
(C) Honesty
(D) Extroversion
(E) Neuroticism

QUESTION 8

Walter Mischel believed that traits vary most based on

(A) circumstance
(B) ethnicity
(C) intelligence
(D) self-efficacy
(E) personal constructs

ANSWERS

1. E
2. A
3. C
4. B
5. D
6. E
7. C
8. A

DEVELOPMENT AND PERSONALITY
Theories and Assessment of Personality

PERSONALITY ASSESSMENT

A PIPE IS NOT JUST A PIPE

Measurements of personality vary according to theoretical orientation.

Psychoanalytic

- Assesses unconscious thoughts and impulses
- Projective tests, such as the Rorschach inkblot test and the Thematic Apperception Test
- Free associaton
- Dream recall

Humanistic

- Relies on interviews to determine levels of self-actualization and honesty with oneself

Social-Cognitive

- Uses scales and questionnaires
- Rotter developed a scale for measuring locus of control
- Other scales have evaluated self-efficacy levels

Trait

- Uses scales and questionnaires
- Eysenck developed the Eysenck Personality Inventory; Cattell developed the 16 Personality Factor Questionnaire
- The Minnesota Multiphasic Personality Inventory, second edition (MMPI-2), is one of the most extensive and widely used inventories; it measures traits and mental disorders, and it includes a lie scale to help compensate for dishonest responses

Behaviorist

- Observe behavior to gather information about personality

According to the **Barnum effect**, people are more likely to rate vague personality characteristics as accurate descriptions of themselves than more personally tailored descriptions. People tend to want to believe in psychics and fortunetellers but should be cautious and skeptical when they are told they have very ambiguous personality traits that could apply to anyone.

BEHAVIORIST THEORIES

WE ARE WHAT WE DO

Behaviorists typically reject other viewpoints regarding personality, arguing that behavior itself is personality. They believe that personality is determined by context: it changes when the environment changes. Few psychologists adhere strictly to this viewpoint; they more likely follow the social-cognitive/cognitive-behavioral theories.

BIOLOGICAL THEORIES

FEELING TEMPERAMENTAL

Biological psychologists believe that personality is shaped by genetics, body chemistry, and body type. These theorists point out that babies appear to have different **temperaments** at birth, and these emotional styles go on to shape future personalities.

Hippocrates (incorrectly) believed that personality is based on varying levels of bodily fluids, called **humors**:

Blood: Cheerful, Hopeful	Phlegm: Calm, Unemotional
Black bile: Sad, Irritable	Yellow bile: Angry, Foul-tempered

Another famous, but empirically unsupported, theory is **William Sheldon's somatotype theory**.

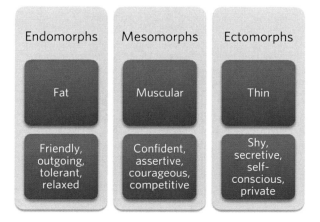

Endomorphs	Mesomorphs	Ectomorphs
Fat	Muscular	Thin
Friendly, outgoing, tolerant, relaxed	Confident, assertive, courageous, competitive	Shy, secretive, self-conscious, private

CRAM QUIZ
Theories and Assessment of Personality

QUESTION 1

Which of the following is not a psychoanalytic measure of personality?

(A) Rorschach
(B) TAT
(C) MMPI
(D) dream recall
(E) free association

QUESTION 2

Which theoretical approach uses the most scales, questionnaires, and inventories to assess personality?

(A) psychoanalytic
(B) humanistic
(C) social-cognitive
(D) trait
(E) behaviorist

QUESTION 3

Which of the following concepts suggests that people are likely to accept vague personality descriptions as accurate representations of themselves?

(A) Hawthorne effect
(B) Barnum effect
(C) Premack principle
(D) Garcia effect
(E) Weber's law

QUESTION 4

Which of the following categories are typically used to describe babies' temperaments?

(A) easy, difficult, slow to warm up
(B) introverted, extroverted, unstable
(C) calm, active, neurotic
(D) agreeable, colicky, despondent
(E) warm, cold, tepid

QUESTION 5

Which of the following is NOT one of Hippocrates' four humors?

(A) blood
(B) black bile
(C) yellow bile
(D) pus
(E) phlegm

QUESTION 6

According to Sheldon's somatotype theory, all of the following characteristics describe mesomorphs EXCEPT

(A) private
(B) confident
(C) assertive
(D) competitive
(E) courageous

QUESTION 7

What theoretical approach suggests that personality changes based on environmental context?

(A) biological
(B) humanistic
(C) psychoanalytic
(D) behaviorist
(E) social-cognitive

QUESTION 8

Which psychologist developed the 16 Personality Factor Questionnaire?

(A) Eysenck
(B) Rotter
(C) Bandura
(D) Rorscach
(E) Cattell

ANSWERS

1. C
2. D
3. B
4. A
5. D
6. A
7. D
8. E

ABNORMAL BEHAVIOR
Theories and Diagnoses of Psychopathology

THEORIES OF ABNORMAL PSYCHOLOGY

BACK TO SCHOOL

As with the other fields of psychology, the different theoretical perspectives approach psychopathology in unique ways. Each group has its own view of the etiology and treatment of psychological disorders.

School of Thought	Cause of Psychological Disorders
Psychoanalytic/ Psychodynamic	Repressed unconscious impulses generally caused by painful or traumatic childhood experiences
Humanistic	Lack of unconditional positive regard; lack of self-awareness; failure to work toward self-actualization
Cognitive	Distorted cognition; illogical thoughts and misinterpretations
Behavioral	Reinforced maladaptive behaviors
Biological	Abnormal brain structure or chemistry
Sociocultural	Society with dysfunctional views of acceptable behavior
Eclectic	Utilizes ideology of multiple theoretical perspectives

DIAGNOSES AND THE DSM-IV-TR

The Diagnostic and Statistical Manual of Mental Disorders, published by the American Psychiatric Association, is currently in its fourth edition, text revised. The DSM is a manual for identifying and classifying the types of psychological illnesses. It provides information about etiology, prevalence rates, and diagnostic criteria. Disorders are listed on five axes:

Axis 1: Main clinical disorders

Axis 2: Personality disorders and mental retardation

Axis 3: Medical conditions that may impact behavior

Axis 4: Psychosocial and environmental stressors

Axis 5: Global assessment of functioning

DEFINING ABNORMALITY

ACHIEVING NORMALCY

One cannot fully understand Abnormal Psychology without asking the question, *What is abnormal?* Psychologists often classify behavior as abnormal using 4 D's: ***deviance, distress, dysfunction, and danger***. Providing a straightforward definition of abnormality is tricky because abnormality is relative, but the definition has several primary characteristics.

- Abnormal behavior is maladaptive, meaning that it interferes with functioning

- Abnormal behavior is disturbing to others and likely to the individual himself

- Abnormal behavior deviates from the statistical norms of society

- Abnormal behavior is considered irrational and unusual by society

Individuals suffering from psychological disorders may meet some or all of these criteria. It is important to keep in mind, though, that what is abnormal is defined by the society in which the behavior occurs—what some societies consider abnormal is perfectly average in other societies.

WHO'S CRAZY HERE ANYWAY?

Psychologist David Rosenhan and several colleagues admitted themselves to mental hospitals, complaining of hearing voices. Each individual was diagnosed with schizophrenia. Once in the hospitals, they acted normally. They did not report hearing any unusual noises and behaved as they usually would in the outside world.

While institutionalized, however, all of their behaviors were seen through the lens of mental illness. Even when these individuals were released, they were diagnosed with schizophrenia in remission.

The Rosenhan study was not perfect in its design, but it raises a valuable point. One should remember that the labels associated with mental illness can be useful for classification, research, and treatment, but they can also be permanently stigmatizing. Above all, one should keep in mind that these labels do not define an individual. A person is more than an illness.

CRAM QUIZ
Theories and Diagnoses of Psychopathology

QUESTION 1

Which theoretical perspective argues that psychological disorders result from reinforced maladaptive behaviors?

- (A) psychoanalytic
- (B) humanistic
- (C) behavioral
- (D) cognitive
- (E) sociocultural

QUESTION 2

According to the biological perspective, psychological disorders result from

- (A) traumatic childhood experiences
- (B) lack of positive regard
- (C) distorted cognition
- (D) dysfunctional societal views
- (E) brain abnormalities

QUESTION 3

Which diagnostic axis is used to classify personality disorders?

- (A) Axis I
- (B) Axis II
- (C) Axis III
- (D) Axis IV
- (E) Axis V

QUESTION 4

Which diagnostic axis provides a numerical ranking on a scale of 0 to 100 of an individual's level of functioning?

- (A) Axis I
- (B) Axis II
- (C) Axis III
- (D) Axis IV
- (E) Axis V

QUESTION 5

Which of the following is NOT one of the four D's used to classify behavior as abnormal?

- (A) danger
- (B) deviance
- (C) dysfunction
- (D) disorder
- (E) distress

QUESTION 6

The stigmatization of psychological labeling is best demonstrated by the

- (A) Milgram study
- (B) Zimbardo study
- (C) Rosenhan study
- (D) Asch study
- (E) Sherif study

QUESTION 7

Dr. Impala is a clinical psychologist who treats individuals with severe psychopathology. When providing therapy, she tailors her approach to the individual client, mixing and matching ideas from a variety of theoretical perspectives. Her approach could best be described as

- (A) humanistic
- (B) sociocultural
- (C) psychodynamic
- (D) eclectic
- (E) haphazard

QUESTION 8

An individual who was diagnosed with schizophrenia but is no longer showing any symptoms is considered

- (A) in remission
- (B) recovered
- (C) undifferentiated
- (D) at risk
- (E) acutely schizophrenic

ANSWERS

1. C
2. E
3. B
4. E
5. D
6. C
7. D
8. A

ABNORMAL BEHAVIOR
Psychological Disorders

ANXIETY AND MOOD DISORDERS

WORRY WART

Anxiety disorders are characterized by intense, persistent tension and worry.

Obsessive Compulsive Disorder
- Characterized by involuntary thoughts and obsessions that cause people to engage in repetitive, maladaptive behaviors called compulsions

Generalized Anxiety Disorder
- Persistent worrying and autonomic nervous system arousal

Anxiety Disorders

Panic Disorder
- Recurring panic attacks characterized by intense fear and physiological discomfort

Postraumatic Stress Disorder
- Anxious response to trauma that results in disturbing memories and flashbacks

Phobias
- Fear or avoidance of specific objects or situations

FEELING BLUE

Mood, or affective, disorders are marked by extreme, unbalanced emotions.

- *Major depressive disorder*: Characterized by two or more weeks of sadness, feelings of worthlessness, and diminished pleasure; typically accompanied by changes in sleep and appetite; this is the most common reason individuals seek psychological treatment
- *Dysthymic disorder*: Symptoms of depression that persist for more than two years
- *Seasonal affective disorder (SAD)*: Symptoms of depression that occur during winter when there is less sunlight
- *Bipolar disorder*: Characterized by alternating periods of depression and mania; in the manic stage, people tend to engage in reckless behavior, feel euphoric, go for long stretches of time without sleep, and speak quickly without inhibition

SCHIZOPHRENIA

BREAK FROM REALITY

Schizophrenia is characterized by a split from reality; its name literally means "split mind." Common symptoms of schizophrenia include delusions, hallucinations, and inappropriate emotional responses. There are five types of schizophrenia: *disorganized, catatonic, paranoid, undifferentiated,* and *residual*.

Symptoms of schizophrenia are divided into two categories:

Positive symptoms
- Indicate the presence of inappropriate thoughts, emotions, and behaviors
- Examples: Hallucinations, delusions, disorganized speech

Negative symptoms
- Indicate the absence of appropriate thoughts, emotions, and behaviors
- Examples: Flat affect, catatonia, apathy, anhedonia

Schizophrenia develops in one of two ways. Process, or *chronic*, schizophrenia has a slow onset. It is usually associated with negative symptoms and has a grimmer prognosis. Reactive, or *acute*, schizophrenia appears as a sudden response to stressors. It is usually associated with positive symptoms and is more likely to be treatable. (Note that positive and negative symptoms do not indicate good or bad, simply the presence or absence of behaviors.)

DISSOCIATIVE DISORDERS

THE OTHER ME

Dissociative disorders involve a loss of memory and identity. They involve separation of awareness from thoughts, feelings, and memories.

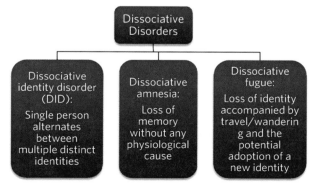

Dissociative Disorders

Dissociative identity disorder (DID):
Single person alternates between multiple distinct identities

Dissociative amnesia:
Loss of memory without any physiological cause

Dissociative fugue:
Loss of identity accompanied by travel/wandering and the potential adoption of a new identity

CRAM QUIZ
Psychological Disorders

QUESTION 1

Which anxiety disorder is characterized by persistent, unwanted thoughts and ritualistic behaviors used to alleviate tension?

(A) generalized anxiety disorder
(B) posttraumatic stress disorder
(C) phobias
(D) obsessive compulsive disorder
(E) panic disorder

QUESTION 2

Which anxiety disorder is most likely to be associated with sudden, intense physiological sensations that resemble a heart-attack?

(A) generalized anxiety disorder
(B) posttraumatic stress disorder
(C) phobias
(D) obsessive compulsive disorder
(E) panic disorder

QUESTION 3

How long must symptoms persist in order for an individual to be classified with major depressive disorder?

(A) one week
(B) two weeks
(C) one month
(D) six months
(E) one year

QUESTION 4

All of the following symptoms typically accompany manic episodes EXCEPT

(A) anhedonia
(B) sleeplessness
(C) euphoria
(D) excessive spending
(E) uninhibited speech

QUESTION 5

Which of the following is NOT one of the types of schizophrenia?

(A) undifferentiated
(B) paranoid
(C) dissociative
(D) residual
(E) catatonic

QUESTION 6

The name *schizophrenia* is derived from two words meaning

(A) multiple personalities
(B) split mind
(C) distorted cognitions
(D) psychotic break
(E) inappropriate emotions

QUESTION 7

Which of the following is NOT a negative symptom of schizophrenia?

(A) flat affect
(B) catatonia
(C) apathy
(D) social withdrawal
(E) disorganized speech

QUESTION 8

Dissociative disorders are most notable for causing loss of

(A) identity
(B) intelligence
(C) bodily control
(D) emotion
(E) weight

ANSWERS

1. D
2. E
3. B
4. A
5. C
6. B
7. E
8. A

ABNORMAL BEHAVIOR
Psychological Disorders (Continued)

PERSONALITY DISORDERS

IT'S NOTHING PERSONAL

Personality disorders include persistent behavioral patterns that impair social functioning.

CLUSTER A: ODD OR ECCENTRIC BEHAVIORS

Paranoid personality disorder

- Suspicious and distrustful of others

Schizoid personality disorder

- Socially detached; lacks emotional range; seems bland and lethargic

Schizotypal personality disorder

- Eccentric; distorted cognition and perception; socially uncomfortable

CLUSTER B: EMOTIONAL OR ERRATIC BEHAVIORS

Antisocial personality disorder

- Lack of empathy, conscience, or remorse; often acts charming and manipulative

Borderline personality disorder

- Unstable mood and relationships; acts impulsively; uncomfortable with self-image and emotions; may engage in self-injury or threaten suicide

Histrionic personality disorder

- Attention-seeking; wants to be liked and accepted; often feels insecure

Narcissistic personality disorder

- Excessive sense of self-importance; egocentric; lack of empathy; attention-seeking

CLUSTER C: ANXIOUS OR FEARFUL BEHAVIORS

Avoidant personality disorder

- Uncomfortable in social or evaluative situations; feels inadequate; sensitive about social perception

Dependent personality disorder

- Extremely submissive in relationships; feels the need to be taken care of

Obsessive compulsive personality disorder

- Needs perfection and control; detail-oriented; moralistic; judgmental

SOMATOFORM DISORDERS

BODILY HARM

Somatoform disorders are physical complaints presented without medical cause.

These theories of personality assume that personality is based on cognitive constructs.

Conversion Disorder	Hypochondriasis	Factitious Disorders
A physiological problem, such as paralysis, occurs as an expression of a psychological problem Freud referred to this as *hysteria*	Irrational preoccupation with having a disease Genuinely concerned about having a serious illness, despite assurances from doctors	Fabrication of symptoms without non-psychological external gain Includes Munchausen's Syndrome and Munchausen's by Proxy

ORGANIC DISORDERS

Organic disorders result from damage to the brain, typically caused by a disease or chemical imbalance. Dementia and Alzheimer's disease are examples of organic disorders.

EATING DISORDERS

Eating disorders are characterized by irrational beliefs about healthy weight and food consumption.

Anorexia Nervosa	Bulimia Nervosa
Refusal to maintain normal weight caused by fear of becoming fat	Unhealthy attitudes and behaviors toward food and weight, without necessarily being underweight

ATTENTION AND CONDUCT DISORDERS

ACTING OUT

Attention deficit hyperactivity disorder (ADHD) causes inattentiveness, distractibility, forgetfulness, fidgeting, and difficulty with organization, among other problems with paying attention and staying still.

Conduct disorder and **oppositional defiant disorder** are other behavioral problems that usually involve violation of social norms and conflict with authority figures.

CRAM QUIZ
Psychological Disorders (Continued)

QUESTION 1

Cluster C personality disorders are characterized as

- (A) eccentric
- (B) erratic
- (C) anxious
- (D) attention-seeking
- (E) detached

QUESTION 2

Christina moves quickly from one relationship to another, her mood fluctuates rapidly, and she often engages in unsafe sex and excessive spending. Christina most likely has

- (A) schizotypal personality disorder
- (B) borderline personality disorder
- (C) antisocial personality disorder
- (D) histrionic personality disorder
- (E) dependent personality disorder

QUESTION 3

Brianna is a perfectionist who spends excessive amounts of time completing projects at work. She often gets into trouble for missing deadlines. She refuses to delegate, claiming that nobody else can do as good a job as she can. Brianna most likely has

- (A) schizoid personality disorder
- (B) histrionic personality disorder
- (C) narcissistic personality disorder
- (D) avoidant personality disorder
- (E) obsessive-compulsive personality disorder

QUESTION 4

A patient goes to the ER with sudden onset of blindness. No physiological cause is found, but it is verified that the patient cannot see. Which of the following problems does the patient most likely have?

- (A) factitious disorder
- (B) hypochondriasis
- (C) conversion disorder
- (D) organic disorder
- (E) traumatic brain injury

QUESTION 5

A baby is brought into the hospital repeatedly for respiratory problems. Doctors cannot find any physical cause. When they review tapes of the baby's room, they discover the mother suffocating the baby. The mother most likely suffers from

- (A) Munchausen's Syndrome by Proxy
- (B) conversion disorder
- (C) hypochondriasis
- (D) antisocial personality disorder
- (E) dissociative identity disorder

QUESTION 6

What is the primary difference between anorexia nervosa and bulimia nervosa?

- (A) amount of food consumed
- (B) severity of cognitive distortion
- (C) associated physical health problems
- (D) weight requirement
- (E) weight loss methods

QUESTION 7

Approximately what percentage of people with anorexia nervosa die as a result of complications from their disease?

- (A) 1%
- (B) 3%
- (C) 5%
- (D) 8%
- (E) 10%

QUESTION 8

Tony has ADHD. All of the following most likely describe his behavior EXCEPT

- (A) forgetful
- (B) violent
- (C) fidgety
- (D) distractible
- (E) disorganized

ANSWERS

1. C
2. B
3. E
4. C
5. A
6. D
7. E
8. B

ABNORMAL BEHAVIOR
Treatment of Psychological Disorders

THERAPEUTIC APPROACHES

COUCH TALK

Psycho-analytic
- Tries to gain insight into the causes of problems, which are likely unconscious
- Uses free association (reporting all thoughts without filtering), hypnosis, and dream analysis
- Encourages transference, in which the patient projects feelings about another person (usually a parent) onto the therapist
- Avoids countertransference, in which the therapist projects feelings onto the patient

Humanistic
- Client-centered therapy
- Tries to help the client achieve self-actualization
- Therapy is non-directive; client chooses his own path rather than being told what to do
- Therapist is open and genuine
- Therapist provides unconditional positive regard and empathic understanding

Behavioral
- May use counterconditioning through aversion therapy or systematic desensitization (replacing anxiey with relaxation in stressful situations)
- *Flooding* is an extinction procedure in which the client is exposed to a frightening stimulus until anxiety is reduced through exposure without negative consequences
- Behavioral contracts and token economies prohibit undersirable behaviors and reward desirable ones

Cognitive and Cognitive-Behavioral
- Rational emotive behavior therapy challenges irrational thoughts, helping to create realistic cause and effect connections between behaviors and consequences
- Cognitive therapy aims to change maladaptive thought processes that lead to depressed views of the self, the world, and the future (cognitive triad)
- Eliminates thinking in which conclusions are drawn without evidence or situations are seen as all-or-nothing

BIOLOGICAL TREATMENTS

SHOCK AND AWE

- *Electroconvulsive therapy*: High voltages of electricity are sent through a patient's head in order to treat severe mental illness that does not respond to therapy or medication; may cause memory loss

- *Psychosurgery*: Physical alteration of the brain, such as a prefrontal lobotomy, in which the frontal lobe is severed from the rest of the brain

- *Psychopharmacology*: Treatment of psychological disorders with medication

DRUGS USED TO TREAT PSYCHOPATHOLOGY

Antipsychotics treat schizophrenia by blocking dopamine receptors. Examples of antipsychotics include Clozapine, Thorazine, and Haldol. These drugs can cause **tardive dyskinesia**, a side effect that results in involuntary movement of the face, tongue, and limbs.

Mood disorders are treated through several kinds of **antidepressants**. *MAO inhibitors* increase serotonin and norepinephrine activity by preventing monoamine oxidase from breaking down neurotransmitters. These drugs require dietary restrictions because some food-drug interactions can be extremely dangerous. *Tryciclic antidepressants* also increase the amount of serotonin and norepinephrine. However, they have generally been replaced with newer antidepressants that have fewer side effects. *Selective serotonin reuptake inhibitors* (SSRIs), such as Prozac, increase the amount of serotonin activity by preventing reuptake. These drugs have fewer side effects than the older antidepressants. *Lithium* is used to treat bipolar disorder but requires careful monitoring, as it is toxic in high doses.

Anxiolytics reduce anxiety levels by depressing the central nervous system. *Barbiturates* are a rarely used type of anxiolytic; they are highly addictive and often interact dangerously with other drugs. *Benzodiazepines*, such as Xanax and Valium, are more commonly used.

GROUP THERAPY

THE MORE, THE MERRIER

Therapy is not always conducted one-on-one. Group therapy may offer additional feedback and support, sometimes at a lower cost. Twelve-step programs have become especially common treatments for substance abuse. Family and couples therapy can help improve communication and resolve relationship problems.

CRAM QUIZ
Treatment of Psychological Disorders

QUESTION 1

Which of the following theoretical perspectives takes a client-centered approach to therapy?

(A) psychoanalytic
(B) humanistic
(C) behavioral
(D) cognitive
(E) biological

QUESTION 2

Which of the following psychologists is incorrectly matched with his mode of therapy?

(A) Beck: cognitive therapy
(B) Ellis: rational emotive behavior therapy
(C) Freud: psychoanalytic
(D) Wolpe: systematic desensitization
(E) Rogers: Gestalt therapy

QUESTION 3

Which therapeutic approach utilizes free association, dream analysis, and hypnosis?

(A) psychoanalytic
(B) humanistic
(C) behavioral
(D) cognitive
(E) biological

QUESTION 4

Which type of therapy aims to eliminate arbitrary inference and dichotomous thinking?

(A) humanistic
(B) existential
(C) cognitive
(D) psychoanalytic
(E) behavioral

QUESTION 5

What is the primary risk associated with electroconvulsive therapy?

(A) tardive dyskinesia
(B) memory loss
(C) blunted affect
(D) hallucinations
(E) vegetative state

QUESTION 6

What neurotransmitter is targeted by antipsychotics?

(A) serotonin
(B) norepinephrine
(C) melatonin
(D) dopamine
(E) monoamine

QUESTION 7

Tardive dyskinesia is most likely to be caused by

(A) antipsychotics
(B) tryciclic antidepressants
(C) SSRIs
(D) benzodiazepines
(E) barbiturates

QUESTION 8

Which of the following drugs is most likely to be used as a treatment for an anxiety disorder?

(A) Wellbutrine
(B) Thorazine
(C) Lithium
(D) Risperdal
(E) Xanax

ANSWERS

1. B
2. E
3. A
4. C
5. B
6. D
7. A
8. E

TEST-TAKING STRATEGY
Test Format and Timing

PACE YOURSELF

WORDS OF WISDOM

In order to do well on the AP test, you need to answer as many questions correctly as possible. That means you need to work fast. But not too fast. Here are some tips to help you find the right balance.

- Wear a watch to keep time yourself; don't rely on other clocks or warnings from a proctor

- You will have two hours to complete the exam: 70 minutes for the multiple-choice and 50 minutes for the free-response

- The test includes 100 multiple-choice questions, so you have less than one minute per question (don't panic!)

- With two essay questions, you will have 25 minutes per response

- Do not rush through the test and make careless mistakes; keep your time restraints in mind, but don't let them scare you

- Start by answering what you know; leave more difficult questions that you need to think about for last

- The test may or may not be organized in order of increasing difficulty, but it doesn't matter; difficulty just has to do with what you have studied, so don't be afraid to skip around

- Keep in mind that easy and hard questions are worth the same number of points

- Remember that no one will ever know your raw score (including you!)

- If you do skip questions, make sure you clearly mark them to come back to and bubble in the correct spot on your answer sheet

- Remember that accuracy is most important; you do not need to finish every question, but you do want to maximize your number of correct answers

- Mark up your test booklet: scribble all over it!

- Once you have eliminated an answer choice, cross it off and don't look back

- Take practice tests; College Board has a lot of sample multiple-choice and free-response questions available, and these can be extremely useful for practicing your pacing, getting a feel for the difficulty of the questions, and possibly even introducing you to some of the same content that will appear on your actual exam

TEST BREAKDOWN

SECTION ONE	SECTION TWO
Multiple-choice	*Free-response*
70 minutes	50 minutes
100 questions	2 questions

SCORING BREAKDOWN

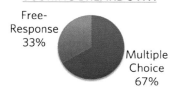

Free-Response 33%

Multiple Choice 67%

CONTENT AREAS

Both sections of the test cover the same 14 areas of psychology:

- History and Approaches (2-4%)
- Research Methods (8-10%)
- Testing and Individual Differences (5-7%)
- Biological Bases of Behavior (8-10%)
- Sensation and Perception (6-8%)
- States of Consciousness (2-4%)
- Learning (7-9%)
- Cognition (8-10%)
- Motivation and Emotion (6-8%)
- Developmental Psychology (7-9%)
- Personality (5-7%)
- Social Psychology (8-10%)
- Abnormal Psychology (7-9%)
- Treatment of Psychological Disorders (5-7%)

SHOULD I GUESS?

On the exam, you receive one point for a correct response and zero points for a blank response. You will be penalized 1/4 of a point for wrong answers. Many students think that if they are not sure of the answer, they shouldn't answer at all, but that's not necessarily the case. If you can eliminate any of the answer choices, you have a decent shot of getting the correct answer and you should guess: one correct guess will make up for four incorrect guesses. But if you have absolutely no idea what the question is talking about and cannot eliminate any answers, you're best not bubbling anything.

TEST-TAKING STRATEGY
Working Your Way Through the Test

MULTIPLE-CHOICE STRATEGIES	FREE-RESPONSE STRATEGIES

A, B, C, D, OR E?

Even if you hate standardized tests (and you wouldn't be alone), you can beat multiple choice questions if you know a little about them.

- Some questions will require basic recall or recognition of factual information while others will require you to apply your knowledge

- The more you know, the quicker and easier the questions will be; study strategies can improve your efficiency and guessing ability, but improving content knowledge is always your best bet

- Make sure you understand what the questions are asking: *read carefully!*

- Watch out for NOT and EXCEPT questions

- Try coming up with the answer yourself before looking at the answer choices; this can save time, prevent second-guessing, and keep you out of traps

- Even so, read through all the answer choices to make sure you pick the BEST possible choice

- Eliminate answer choices you know are wrong so you can spend more time focusing on the rest

- Get rid of answer choices that appear too extreme, don't make any sense, or don't seem to fit in with any of the other options

- When "all of the above" is an option, it may very well be correct: if two of the answers look right, but you're not sure about the others, consider guessing "all of the above"

- If you are unsure of an answer at first, leave the question and come back to it later; you might find the answer in another portion of the test

- If you finish all the questions you are sure about and still have some extra time at the end, don't just sit there! Brainstorm everything you know about questions that look unfamiliar, and the information just might come to you

- Try not to overanalyze the questions; if a question seems really easy, that does NOT mean it is a trick

- Look over your answer sheet at the end of the test and make sure the bubbles are filled in neatly; don't lose points for partially filled bubbles that don't register or stray marks that make it look like you chose two answers

- Have four C's in a row? Don't worry, the pattern of your responses probably doesn't mean anything; focus more on the content than the letters of the choices

NO MORE BUBBLES

The concept of writing an essay about what you've learned may be scary at first, but just put on your thinking cap and show what you've learned!

- First, make sure you understand what the question is asking; don't get halfway through your essay to realize that you've been writing about the wrong thing all along!

- Answer all parts of the question

- Follow directions! If the directions tell you to discuss, define, or compare/contrast, do it!

- If the prompt implies organization, follow it (but without labeling the parts of your essay A, B, C, D)

- AP essay graders are looking for you to provide certain points of content information; try to guess the rubric based on the question and create an outline of what points you plan to address before you start writing

- Make sure you rewrite your outline points in full sentences with proper paragraphs: pure outlines will not receive credit

- Do not bother restating the question

- You do not need to write a lengthy introduction or conclusion; you will not earn extra points for a literary masterpiece, so get to the point quickly

- Providing additional information that is not asked for in order to prove your knowledge of psychology won't help: you will not receive extra points for unrelated content, and you'll lose precious time

- As long as you don't contradict yourself, incorrect information will not be penalized; graders generally only give points rather than take them away

- When you use terms and examples (you should!) make sure you define and explain them clearly

- Try to support all your statements with an example or study, not something from your personal life or favorite soap opera

- Use trigger and transitional words that help graders to spot key points and examples

- Try your best to write legibly; if the grader cannot read what you write, he cannot give you points for writing it

- Keep in mind that graders are reading hundreds of essays; in each one, they are simply trying to determine how many pieces of information from their rubric are included in your essay

CRUNCH KIT
AP Psychology in Four Pages (Page 1)

HISTORY OF PSYCHOLOGY

- Wilhelm Wundt became the founder of scientific psychology after opening a lab in Germany in 1879
- Wundt and Edward Titchener developed a school of thought known as structuralism, which focused on breaking mental processes down into their components
- William James authored the first psychology textbook and developed functionalism
- Functionalism was based on the theory of natural selection and focused on the adaptive qualities of mental processes and behaviors

APPROACHES TO PSYCHOLOGY

- *Biopsychology:* physiology and behavior
- *Behaviorism:* observable behaviors
- *Cognitive:* mental processes
- *Evolutionary:* adaptive qualities of behavior
- *Humanistic:* impact of free will and personal values on behavior
- *Psychoanalytic/Psychodynamic:* influence of the unconscious mind on thoughts and behaviors
- *Gestalt:* whole experiences are more than the sum of their parts

RESEARCH METHODS AND STATISTICS

- *Experiment:* an independent variable is manipulated in order to determine its effect on a dependent variable
- *Survey:* compile data from questionnaires to determine the relationship between variables
- *Case study:* study a single individual or event in depth
- *Naturalistic observation:* view participants in their usual environments
- *Sampling:* the process of choosing research participants
- A representative sample has roughly the same demographics as the population, while a random sample allows every member of the population an equal opportunity of being chosen
- *Assignment:* the division of research participants into groups; random assignment allows every participant an equal chance of being selected for either the experimental or control group
- A research measure is valid if it measures what was intended; it is reliable if it can be duplicated to get the same results consistently
- Correlations measure the degree of association between two variables; correlations range from -1 to +1
- Variability describes clustering of numbers in a data set
- Standard deviation is a measure of variability based on the average distance between data points and the mean
- The null hypothesis states that experimental treatment did not have an effect; the alternative hypothesis states that treatment did have an effect
- Statistical significance suggests that a result of research likely did not occur by chance alone

INTELLIGENCE

- Alfred Binet created the first IQ test
- The original IQ was calculated as the ratio of mental age over chronological age, multiplied by 100; IQ is now determined by comparing scores to same-aged peers
- An IQ of 100 is considered average; scores of 135 and over are labeled gifted; scores of 70 and below are labeled mentally retarded
- Charles Spearman argued that intelligence is a single factor; specific abilities underlie one common ability
- Sternberg believed there were three types of intelligence: analytical, practical, and creative
- Gardner identified eight types of intelligence: linguistic, logical-mathematical, musical, spatial, kinesthetic, environmental, interpersonal, intrapersonal

NERVOUS SYSTEM, NEURON, NEURAL TRANSMISSION

- *Central nervous system:* brain and spinal cord
- *Peripheral nervous system:* all other nerves; carries messages between CNS and the rest of the body
- *Sensory/afferent neurons:* sends information to brain
- *Motor/efferent neurons:* carries information from brain
- *Autonomic nervous system:* controls involuntary movement
- *Somatic nervous system:* controls voluntary movement
- *Sympathetic nervous system:* part of ANS; controls fight or flight response
- *Parasympathetic nervous system:* part of ANS; conserves energy
- Dendrites receive information from other neurons
- Axons send information to other neurons
- Axons are coated with a myelin sheath, which accelerates neural transmission
- The gap between neurons is the synapse
- Nerves carry messages within and between cells when a threshold of stimulation is reached
- Neural transmission follows the all-or-none principle: nerves either fire or they don't; strength of firing is fixed
- Neurotransmitters are chemicals messengers that carry information between cells; when they are done, the chemicals are broken down by enzymes or absorbed back into the cells

ANATOMY OF THE BRAIN

- The hindbrain is the oldest part; controls basic biological functions; includes cerebellum, medulla oblongata, reticular activating system, pons, and thalamus
- The midbrain is the second oldest part of the brain; made up of structures between the spinal cord and forebrain; integrates muscle movements and sensory information; includes hippocampus, amygdala, and hypothalamus
- Forebrain: newest part; runs higher cognitive functions; includes frontal lobe (executive functions), parietal lobe (touch), temporal lobe (auditory), occipital lobe (visual)

CRUNCH KIT
AP Psychology in Four Pages (Page 2)

BRAIN IMAGING

- EEGs record the electrical activity of neurons in the brain
- MRIs use magnetic fields and radio waves to create pictures of the brain; fMRIs use successive scans to compare blood flow and monitor brain activity
- CT scans build a picture of the brain by putting together a series of X rays
- PET scans detect the movement of glucose in the brain, which shows what parts are most active

ENDOCRINE SYSTEM

- Sends information around the body through hormones
- Hormones are slower than neurotransmitters
- The pituitary gland triggers other glands; the pineal gland controls sleep/wake cycle; the thyroid gland regulates metabolism; the pancreas produces insulin; the ovaries and testes control sex hormones

GENETICS

- Humans have 46 chromosomes, half from each parent
- Dominant traits require only one copy of a gene to be expressed; recessive traits require two copies of the gene to be expressed
- Genotype is an individual's genetic makeup; phenotype is an individual's appearance
- Down syndrome is caused by an extra 21st chromosome; it often causes mental retardation
- Turner's and Klinefelter's syndromes involve abnormal sex chromosomes
- Identical/monozygotic twins share 100% of their genetic material, while fraternal/dizygotic twins were implanted simultaneously but do not have the same DNA

VISION

- *Cornea:* focuses light and protects the outer eye
- *Pupil:* dilates and contracts to determine how much light passes through
- *Rods:* black and white vision; peripheral vision
- *Cones:* color vision; primarily located in the fovea
- *Distal stimulus:* the object in the environment; proximal stimulus: the image of an object as it is projected on the retina
- *Trichromatic theory of color vision:* the eye has receptors for the primary colors of light—red, green, and blue
- *Opponent process theory of color vision:* cells are stimulated and inhibited by opposite colors; opposing colors are red and green, yellow and blue, and white and black
- The law of Pragnanz states that people perceive objects in the simplest and most orderly way possible; objects are grouped accorded to proximity, closure, similarity, and continuity
- Bottom-up processing identifies objects by breaking them down into their component parts; top-down processing relies on prior experience to identify objects

HEARING

- Sound waves enter the ear through the pinna; they travel through to the tympanic membrane, which vibrates when hit by the waves; the eardrum is attached to three bones: the hammer, anvil, and stirrup
- Vibrations pass through the oval window to the cochlea, to the auditory nerve, and then to the temporal lobe
- The amplitude of sound waves determines their loudness
- The frequency of sound waves determines their pitch
- Frequency theory posits that low-pitched sounds can be explained by the rate of hair cells firing in the cochlea
- Place theory suggests that high and low pitches are produced depending on where sound waves are generated within the cochlea
- Conduction deafness is caused by damage in the middle or outer ear; sensorineural deafness results from damage to the cochlea or auditory cortex

SENSORY THRESHOLDS

- *Absolute threshold:* minimal amount of stimulation necessary to detect a stimulus at least half the time
- *Just noticeable difference:* minimum distance between stimuli necessary to detect them as distinct
- *Weber's law:* the difference threshold is proportional to the intensity of the stimulus

ATTENTION

- Selective attention involves focusing on one thing while ignoring another
- *Cocktail party phenomenon:* one can hear one's name mentioned in another conversation; individuals filter information even when focusing elsewhere
- Divided attention involves attempting to focus on multiple things simultaneously

SLEEP

- Sleep occurs in five stages; REM sleep is the stage associated with dreaming
- Dreams may explain what is happening to the body during sleep (activation-synthesis theory) or process experiences from the preceding day (information-processing theory)
- *Insomnia:* persistent difficulty falling or staying asleep
- *Narcolepsy:* inability to stay awake
- *Night terrors:* extreme fear during sleep that is rarely remembered upon waking
- *Sleepwalking:* wandering around and performing other activities while asleep

SUBSTANCE USE

- *Abuse:* distress or impairment in functioning
- *Dependence:* physical and psychological reliance
- *Tolerance:* needing more of a substance to achieve the same effect
- *Withdrawal:* symptoms that occur as a result of stopping substance use

CRUNCH KIT
AP Psychology in Four Pages (Page 3)

CLASSICAL CONDITIONING

- An unconditioned stimulus is joined with a neutral stimulus to elicit a conditioned response
- Acquisition occurs when the stimuli are paired; extinction occurs when the response disappears after the conditioned stimulus is repeatedly presented without the unconditioned stimulus
- When subjects respond to stimuli similar to the conditioned stimulus, it is called generalization; when they can differentiate between closely related stimuli, it is called discrimination
- In the Little Albert study, John Watson conditioned a baby to fear white rats by pairing them with loud noises
- John Garcia discovered that taste aversion can be conditioned by pairing a food or drink with nausea

OPERANT CONDITIONING

- Behaviors that produce a pleasant consequence are likely to be repeated
- Reinforcement strengthens the likelihood of repeating a response; punishment decreases it
- Continuous reinforcement rewards every correct response; intermittent reinforcement rewards either a certain number of responses or rewards after a certain period of time

OTHER TYPES OF LEARNING

- Observational learning occurs by watching and imitating
- Latent learning is knowledge that is not demonstrated until reinforcement is provided
- Insight learning is a sudden realization of how to solve a problem
- Abstract learning involves understanding concepts, which are rules for organizing stimuli into groups

MEMORY AND FORGETTING

- Short-term memory holds seven items for about 30 seconds
- Long-term memory can store encoded information permanently
- Working memory involves storing and manipulating information in the short-term memory
- Sensory memory for auditory information is echoic, while it is iconic for visual information
- Retroactive interference occurs when new information interferes with the ability to recall old information; proactive interference occurs when old information interferes with the ability to recall new information
- Amnesia is the inability to remember information, usually caused by psychological trauma or brain injury

PROBLEM SOLVING

- A heuristic is a rule of thumb used to make a quick judgment; an algorithm is a rule that determines guaranteed answers
- Functional fixedness is the tendency to use objects only for their designated purpose

PROBLEM SOLVING (CONTINUED)

- People usually look for information that confirms their viewpoints (confirmation bias) and are unwilling to accept contradictory evidence (belief perseverance)

LANGUAGE

- *Phonemes:* smallest units of sound; *morphemes:* smallest meaningful units of sound; *syntax:* word order; *semantics:* word meanings; *pragmatics:* appropriate use of language based on context
- *Surface structure:* the arrangement of words; *deep structure:* word connotation
- *Holophrases:* single words that convey broad meaning
- *Telegraphic speech:* a combination of several words without connecting articles

MOTIVATION

- *Drive reduction theory:* people are motivated to meet biological needs and achieve homeostasis
- *Instinct theory:* people perform inborn species-specific behaviors necessary for survival
- *Incentive theory:* people perform behaviors based on their desire for rewards
- *Opponents process theory:* people try to stay at a baseline level of motivation
- *Arousal theory:* people try to achieve a balanced level of excitement; the Yerkes-Dodson law states that people perform best at a medium level of arousal
- *Social theory:* people respond to social pressures
- *Maslow's hierarchy of needs:* survival and physiological needs, safety and security, belongingness and love, self-esteem, and self-actualization
- *Stages of the sexual response cycle:* excitement, plateau, orgasm, resolution
- *Set-point theory:* the hypothalamus maintains the body's optimum weight through metabolic rate

THEORIES OF EMOTION AND STRESS

- *James-Lange:* physiological change causes emotion
- *Cannon-Bard:* physiological changes and emotional experiences occur at the same time
- *Two-factor:* physiological changes occur, followed by cognitive labeling of the emotional state
- Hans Selye developed the general adaptation syndrome (GAS) to describe individuals' response to stressors
- *Stages of GAS:* alarm, resistance, exhaustion

SOCIAL PSYCHOLOGY

- *Social loafing:* the tendency to exert less effort on group tasks; social facilitation: improved performance of well-learned tasks in the presence of others
- *Groupthink:* group members agree to preserve group harmony; *group polarization:* the dominant opinion gains strength through discussion

CRUNCH KIT
AP Psychology in Four Pages (Page 4)

SOCIAL PSYCHOLOGY (CONTINUED)

- *Fundamental attribution error:* tendency to infer that others' actions reflect dispositions more than situations
- *Self-serving bias:* tendency to attribute success to disposition and to blame failure on circumstance
- Attraction increases based on similarity, proximity, and reciprocal liking
- Persuasion through the central route focuses on content, while the peripheral route is based on the characteristics of the communicator
- Cognitive dissonance results from a conflict between attitudes and behaviors
- Instrumental aggression is used to gain something; hostile aggression lacks a clear purpose but is usually emotional and impulsive
- Bystander intervention is the influence of nearby people on the likelihood of performing helping behaviors
- The more people around when help is needed, the less each person feels responsible to help (diffusion of responsibility)
- Stereotypes are prototypes of people based on reputedly common attributes of group members
- Prejudice is a negative attitude about a group of people without evidence
- Discrimination involves acting on prejudice by treating members of a stereotypes group poorly
- Obedience involves following the instructions of authority figures without questioning
- Compliance involves doing as asked, even against one's self-interest
- Conformity is change to fit in with members of a group

DEVELOPMENTAL PSYCHOLOGY

- Stages of prenatal development: zygote, embryo, fetus
- Mary Ainsworth found three styles of attachment by observing infants in strange situations; most displayed secure attachment, while others were avoidant and resistant
- Piaget's stages of cognitive development: sensorimotor, preoperational, concrete operational, formal operational
- Freud's psychosexual stages include oral, anal, phallic, latency, and genital
- Vygotsky devised the concept of a zone of proximal development, the range between what children can do by themselves and what they can do with help
- *Erikson's developmental tasks:* trust vs. mistrust, autonomy vs. shame and doubt, initiative vs. guilt, industry vs. inferiority, identity vs. role confusion, intimacy vs. isolation, generativity vs. stagnation, integrity vs. despair
- *Kohlberg's stages of morality:* preconventional, conventional, postconventional
- Gender identity develops by age three; gender typing and constancy develop between ages two and seven

PERSONALITY

- Freud divided personality into the id (survival), ego (reality), and superego (conscience)
- Defense mechanisms reduce anxiety from conflict between the id and ego
- Jung believed that people have a personal unconscious and collective unconscious
- Alder thought that people develop feelings of inferiority but can overcome them through community service
- Rogers believed that self-concept is strongest when people are treated with unconditional positive regard
- Bandura posited that personality is based on self-efficacy
- Rotter believed that people either have an internal locus of control and attribute successes and failures to their own efforts or an external locus of control and believe that successes and failures result from chance
- The Big Five traits are openness, conscientiousness, extroversion, agreeableness, and neuroticism
- Mischel argued that traits depend on circumstance
- Personality can be assessed through projective tests, such as the Rorschach inkblot test and the Thematic Apperception Test, or through scales, questionnaires, behavioral observations, and interviews

CAUSES OF PSYCHOLOGICAL DISORDERS

- *Psychoanalytic:* repressed unconscious impulses
- *Humanistic:* lack of unconditional positive regard and self-awareness
- *Cognitive:* distorted and illogical thoughts
- *Behavioral:* reinforced maladaptive behaviors
- *Biological:* abnormal brain structure or chemistry
- *Sociocultural:* dysfunctional societal views

DIAGNOSES, DISORDERS, AND TREATMENT

- Diagnoses are based on the Diagnostic and Statistical Manual of Mental Disorders (DSM-IV-TR), which has a five-axis system of classifying disorders
- Abnormality is defined by the 4 D's: deviance, distress, dysfunction, and danger
- *Anxiety disorders:* persistent tension and worry
- *Mood disorders:* extreme, unbalanced emotions
- *Schizophrenia:* a split from reality, including delusions, hallucinations, and inappropriate emotional responses
- *Dissociative disorders:* loss of memory and identity
- *Personality disorders:* persistent behavioral patterns that impair social functioning
- *Somatoform disorders:* physical problems without medical cause
- *Eating disorders:* irrational beliefs about weight and food
- Treatment involves therapy, medication, and (rarely) electroconvulsive therapy or psychosurgery
- Medications include antipsychotics, antidepressants (MAO inhibitors, tricyclics, SSRIs), and anxiolytics

CRUNCH KIT
List of Lists

20 FAMOUS FIGURES

Bandura, Albert	Studied social-learning theory
Binet, Alfred	Created the first intelligence test
Calkins, Mary	First female president of the APA
Chomsky, Noam	Researched language acquisition
Erikson, Erik	Developed psychosocial stage theory
Freud, Sigmund	Developed psychoanalytic theory
James, Williams	Published psychology's first textbook
Kinsey, Alfred	Surveyed human sexual behavior
Kohlberg, Lawrence	Created a stage theory of moral development
Maslow, Abraham	Created the hierarchy of needs
Piaget, Jean	Devised theory of cognitive development
Rogers, Carl	Developed client-centered therapy
Skinner, B.F.	Invented Skinner box to study reinforcement
Spearman, Charles	Developed concept of general intelligence
Thorndike, Edward	Developed the law of effect
Titchener, Edward	Brought psychology to America
Vygotsky, Lev	Studied the zone of proximal development
Washburn, Margaret Floy	First woman to be granted a doctorate in psychology; second female president of APA
Watson, John	Considered the father of behaviorism

20 LOWER-PRIORITY PEOPLE

Baumrind, Diana	Researched styles of parenting and discipline
Costa & McCrae	Listed Big Five traits of personality
Dix, Dorothea	Advocated for improved asylum conditions
Ebbinghaus, Herman	Studied the influence of repetition on learning nonsense syllables
Fechner, Gustav	Developed the field of psychophysics
Festinger, Leon	Studied cognitive dissonance
Galton, Francis	Applied theories of evolution to intelligence
Garcia, John	Studied conditioned taste aversion
Gardner, Howard	Created theory of multiple intelligences
Gilligan, Carol	Criticized gender bias of Kohlberg's study
Hall, G. Stanley	Described adolescence as a time of "storm and stress"
Hilgard, Ernest	Researched hypnotic dissociation
Loftus, Elizabeth	Studied reconstructed memory and eyewitness testimony
Miller, George	Discovered capacity of short-term memory
Pinel, Phillipe	Argued for moral treatment of mentally ill
Rescorla, Robert	Believed animals could learn to predict events
Selye, Hans	Described general adaptation syndrome
Sternberg, Robert	Devised triarchic theory of intelligence
Weber, Ernst	Discovered the just noticeable difference

10 SCHOOLS OF THOUGHT

Behaviorism	Emphasizes the connection between antecedent, behavior, and consequence (Thorndike, Skinner, Watson, Pavlov)
Biopsychology	Studies the relationships between physiology and behavior; examines the extent to which genetic predisposition influences behavior
Cognitive	Looks at the brain as an information processor like a computer (Piaget, Chomsky)
Evolutionary	Sees behavior as adaptive; based on Darwin's theory of natural selection
Functionalism	Focused on the adaptive qualities of mental processes and behaviors (James)
Gestalt	Whole experiences are viewed as more than the sum of their individual parts (Wertheimer)
Humanistic	Believes people are inherently good; behavior is influenced by free will and personal values (Rogers, Maslow)
Psychoanalytic and Psychodynamic	Thinks thoughts and behaviors are influenced by the unconscious mind; childhood experiences have a long-lasting impact on the development of adult personality and psychological disorders (Freud, Jung, Adler)
Structuralism	Broke mental processes down into basic components (Wundt, Titchener)

12 JOBS IN PSYCHOLOGY

Clinical psychologist	Researches, assesses, and treats people with psychological disorders
Cognitive psychologist	Researches mental processes such as perception, memory, and problem-solving
Counseling psychologist	Provides therapy for life problems (school, work, relationships) and personal growth
Developmental psychologist	Researches the development of mental processes and behaviors across the lifespan
Educational psychologist	Applies psychological assessment to improve children's development in school
Human factors psychologist	Redesigns products to make them more intuitive and effective for consumer use
Industrial-Organizational psychologist	Studies methods of increasing employee productivity and comfort in the workplace by boosting morale and efficiency
Personality psychologist	Studies individual differences in traits, preferences, and inclinations
Physiological psychologist	Studies brain and brain-body interactions
Psychiatrist	Medical doctor; treats psychological disorders through medication
Psychometrician	Creates methods of psychological assessment
Social psychologist	Interested in how people and groups interact and function together

CRUNCH KIT
List of Lists

ETHICAL PRINCIPLES

Beneficence and nonmalifence	Psychologists must try to help, not harm, the people with whom they work
Confidentiality	People have a right to keep information between themselves and their therapist unless the person is a threat to themselves or others or reveals evidence of abuse to vulnerable persons
Debriefing	After participating in research, researchers must explain the study and ensure that no one was harmed
Fidelity and responsibility	Psychologists should uphold the standards of conduct and minimize conflicts of interest
Informed consent	Research participants must be informed of the risks and benefits involved in a study
Institutional Review Board	Assesses research plans to determine whether they meet ethical guidelines
Integrity	Psychologists should promote accuracy, honesty, and truthfulness
Justice	Psychologists must allow all people equal access to psychological services and contributions
Respect for rights and dignity	Psychologists must respect people's rights to dignity, privacy, confidentiality, and self-determination

PSYCHOLOGICAL RESEARCH

Case study	Detailed research focusing on a single person or situation
Correlation	Measure of how closely related two sets of variables are, ranging from -1 to +1
Empiricism	Knowledge results from sensory experience; science should be performed through experimentation and observation
Experiment	Manipulation of one variable in order to observe the impact on another variable
Fact	Verifiable observation that is consistent across observers
Hypothesis	Testable prediction made to explain observations in order to validate, reject, or revise a theory
Naturalistic observation	Watching and recording organisms in their natural environment
Operational definition	Statement of how research variables are measured or manipulated
Survey	Collecting self-reported information about beliefs, attitudes, preferences, or activities
Theory	Strongly supported explanation that organizes and predicts behaviors and events; a means of interpreting facts, but not a completely verifiable truth

STATISTICS 101

Confounding variable	Variable other than those intentionally studied that might be responsible for results
Dependent variable	Experimental variable that changes in response to manipulation of the other variable
Descriptive stats	Provide organized overview of data
Independent variable	Experimental variable that is manipulated in order to produce a measurable effect on the other factor
Inferential stats	Interpret and draw conclusions from data
Mean	Average of scores in a distribution
Median	Number located in the center of a distribution
Mode	Most frequently represented number in a distribution
Normal curve	Bell-shaped distribution with most scores in the middle and fewer at the outer edges; has the same mean, median, and mode
Range	Distance between the lowest and highest scores in a distribution
Reliability	Extent to which test results are consistent under similar conditions at different times
Standard deviation	Measurement of the variability between scores in a data set
Validity	Extent to which a test measures what it is intended to measure

ASSESSMENT AND TESTING

Achievement test	Determines amount of knowledge previously learned (AP tests, for example)
Aptitude test	Determines abilities and potential; predicts capacity to learn and perform in the future (college entrance exams, for example)
Minnesota Multiphasic Personality Inventory (MMPI)	Measures traits and mental disorders; one of the most extensively used personality inventories; includes a lie scale to compensate for the dishonesty inherent in self-report measures
Power test	Determines ability to answer questions of increasing difficulty
Rorschach inkblot test	Reveals personality by interpreting 10 ambiguous inkblots
Speed test	Determines how quickly one can answer a large number of questions in an insufficient time period
Stanford-Binet IQ test	First test of intelligence; created for French schoolchildren; modified by Terman for use in America
Thematic Apperception Test	Reveals personality by making up stories to accompany a series of pictures
Wechsler's intelligence scales	Most common modern intelligence tests; include Wechsler Adult Intelligence Scale (WAIS), Wechsler Intelligence Scale for Children (WISC), and Wechsler Preschool and Primary Scale of Intelligence (WPPSI)

CRUNCH KIT
List of Lists

NEUROANATOMY IN BRIEF

Amygdala	Controls emotions of fear, anger, and aggression
Basal ganglia	Planning and producing movement
Broca's area	Language expression; located in frontal lobe
Cerebellum	Movement and balance; sensory processing
Forebrain	Involved in higher level cognitive functions
Hindbrain	Controls basic biological functions
Hippocampus	Memory formation
Hypothalamus	Temperature, hunger/thirst, sexual arousal, endocrine system
Lobes	Frontal: executive functions; parietal: touch, pain; temporal: hearing; occipital: vision
Medulla oblongata	Breathing, digestion, heart rate, blood pressure, swallowing
Midbrain	Integrates muscle movement and sensory information
Reticular formation	Wakefulness and alertness
Thalamus	Conveys information between visual and auditory systems
Wernicke's area	Language comprehension and expression; located in temporal lobe

REVISITING THE NERVOUS SYSTEM

Central nervous system (CNS)	Nerves located in brain and spinal cord; control center
Peripheral NS	Nerves running through the body; includes autonomic NS and somatic NS
Autonomic NS	Controls glands and internal organs; includes sympathetic NS and parasympathetic NS
Somatic NS	Enables control of skeletal muscles
Parasympathetic NS	Conserves energy; calms internal systems down when body is not threatened
Sympathetic NS	Mobilizes body for fight or flight response
Sensory neuron	Sends information to the CNS from tissues
Motor neuron	Sends information from CNS to tissues
Interneuron	Conveys information within the CNS
Axon	Sends information to other neurons
Dendrite	Receives information from other cells
Myelin sheath	Encases axon to speed up neural impulses
Synapse	Gap between axon and dendrite
Action potential	Neural impulses triggered by positively charged ions traveling through the axon
All or none principle	Sufficiently stimulated neuron will fire as long as threshold is reached
Reuptake	Reabsorption of excess neurotransmitters

THE FIVE SENSES (AND BEYOND)

Cornea	Protects outer eye and focuses light
Pupil	Dilates and contracts to control light entry
Retina	Converts light into neural impulses
Cones	Responsible for color perception
Rods	Responsible for seeing black, white, and gray
Depth perception	Ability to gauge distance and see in 3-D
Middle ear	Transmits auditory information from the eardrum to the cochlea
Cochlea	Transmits auditory information to temporal lobe
Eardrum	Vibrates when hit by sound waves; attached to three bones: hammer, anvil, and stirrup
Taste buds	Receptors on tongue that determine whether a substance tastes sweet, sour, salty, or bitter
Tactical receptors	Provide information about pressure, pain, and temperature
Gate-control theory	High-priority pain messages temporarily prevent transmission of low-priority messages
Smell	Receptors in the nose absorb smells and send information to the limbic system
Vestibular sense	Informs body of orientation and balance
Kinesthetic sense	Tracks where specific body parts are located and how they are oriented
Transduction	Conversion of stimulus into action potential

PRINCIPLES OF LEARNING

Classical conditioning	Association of a neutral stimulus with a stimulus that causes a natural response
Operant conditioning	Association of a behavior with its consequence (reward or punishment)
Reinforcement	Strengthening of a behavior by rewarding it with a pleasurable stimulus (positive) or removing an unpleasant stimulus (negative)
Punishment	Decreasing the likelihood of a behavior with an aversive consequence
Law of effect	More likely to repeat behaviors with pleasant consequences than unpleasant ones
Continuous reinforcement	Reward every correct response; learning and extinction occur quickly
Intermittent reinforcement	Rewards given after a specified number of responses occur or a time period has elapsed
Shaping	Reinforcement of successive approximations of desired behavior
Taste aversion	Conditioning food/drink avoidance by pairing it with an unconditioned stimulus that causes nausea or vomiting
Observational learning	Learning by watching and imitating others; also called social and vicarious learning
Insight learning	Learning by sudden understanding
Latent learning	Learning by experience that is not demonstrated without incentive
Abstract learning	Conceptual understanding; organize stimuli

CRUNCH KIT
List of Lists

MEMORY IN A FLASH

Amnesia	Loss of memory from injury or trauma
Echoic memory	Auditory information held very briefly
Encoding	Process of entering information in memory
Episodic memory	Memory for personal events
Iconic memory	Photographic image of visual information
Implicit memory	Involuntarily recalled behavioral memories
Long-term	Memory for large amounts of information that can be stored permanently
Mnemonic	Memory aid using imagery and organization
Proactive interference	Inability to learn new information because of disruptive old information
Retrieval	Process of accessing information
Retroactive interference	Inability to remember old information because of disruptive new information
Semantic memory	Memory for word meanings, concepts, and general information
Serial position effect	Tendency to remember first and last items in a list better than those in the middle
Short-term	Brief memory for five to nine items
Storage	Process of retaining information in memory
Working memory	Memory used for temporary storage and the manipulation of information

INTRO LINGUISTICS

Babbling	Use of phonemes that convey meaning
Concepts	Rules for organizing stimuli into groups
Cooing	Use of phonemes that do not resemble real words
Deep structure	Connotation of words
Holophrases	Single words that convey broad meanings
Language acquisition device	Innate ability to learn language with sufficient exposure during critical period
Linguistic relativity	Theory that language controls cognition
Morpheme	Smallest meaningful unit of language
Overextension	Misuse of a word to describe similar stimuli in the same category
Overgeneralization	Misapplication of grammar rules
Phoneme	Smallest unit of sound
Pragmatics	Impact of context on language meaning
Semantics	Study of word and sentence meanings
Surface structure	Arrangement of words
Syntax	Rules for ordering words into sentences
Telegraphic speech	Early language that omits auxiliary words
Transformational grammar	System of organizing language according to surface and deep structures

SOCIAL PSYCH MADE EASY

Aggression	Hurtful behavior performed out of anger or as a means to an end
Altruism	Selfless concern for others
Bystander effect	Decreased likelihood of offering help when others are present
Cognitive dissonance	People change beliefs or actions to reduce discomfort from conflicting thoughts
Conformity	Pressure to act like other group members
Deindividuation	Abandonment of self-awareness in a group
Discrimination	Negative action toward members of a group
Door-in-the-face	Tendency to agree to a small request after turning down a large one
Foot-in-the-door	Tendency to agree to a large request after agreeing to a small one
Fundamental attribution error	Overestimating the impact of disposition on other people's behavior
Group polarization	Strengthening of dominant group opinion
Groupthink	Implicit agreement to minimize conflict
Prejudice	Unjustified negative beliefs about people
Self-fulfilling prophecy	Influence of expectations on future behaviors
Social facilitation	Improved performance in presence of others
Social loafing	Tendency to exert less effort on a group task
Stereotype	Overgeneralization of a group of people

WOMB TO TOMB IN 15 TERMS

Moro reflex	When startled, babies fling out their limbs
Babinski reflex	Stroking the bottom of a baby's foot causes toes to splay
Attachment styles	Secure, avoidant, resistant
Parenting styles	Permissive, authoritative, authoritarian
Sensorimotor	Develop object permanence and motor skills
Preoperational	Develop symbolic thought and language
Concrete operational	Develop understanding of conservation
Formal operational	Develop abstract thought and metacognition
Psychosexual stages	Development based on erogenous zones: oral, anal, phallic, latency, genital (Freud)
Zone of proximal development	Range between what children can do alone and with help (Vygotsky)
Psychosocial development	Development based on passing through a series of crises (Erikson)
Preconventional morality	Moral choices based on self-interest; avoid punishment and try to earn rewards
Conventional morality	Moral decisions based on law and convention; internalize societal rules
Postconventional morality	Moral decisions based on personal values of what is right, fair, and ethical, even if it goes against law and social rules
Gender development	Learn to label own gender, fulfill sex-related roles, and understand that gender is fixed

CRUNCH KIT
List of Lists

APPROACHING PERSONALITY

Big Five traits	Openness, conscientiousness, extroversion, agreeableness, neuroticism
Collective unconscious	Memory of all the experiences in a species' history (Jung)
Defense mechanisms	Unconscious distortion of reality in order to reduce anxiety
Ego	Part of personality that mediates between desires for pleasure and perfection
Fixation	Focus on unresolved psychosexual stages
Id	Part of personality that wants instant gratification
Identification	Children's attempt to incorporate rival (same-sex) parent's values
Locus of control	Perception of control over one's own fate
Oedipus complex	Boy's jealousy of his father and sexual desire for his mother
Self-actualization	Fulfillment of individual potential (Maslow)
Self-efficacy	Person's perception of his own abilities
Superego	Part of personality that strives for idealism
Traits	Stable characteristics that predispose individuals to behave in a particular way
Unconditional positive regard	Complete acceptance of another person despite their imperfections (Rogers)

TREATMENTS FOR PSYCHOLOGICAL DISORDERS

Active listening	Restatement and clarification of statements
Antidepressants	Treat depression and elevate mood by influencing serotonin activity; includes MAO inhibitors, tricyclics, and SSRIs
Antipsychotics	Treat schizophrenia by blocking dopamine receptors; include Clozapine, Thorazine, and Haldol; may cause tardive dyskinesia
Anxiolytics	Reduce anxiety levels by depressing the CNS; includes Xanax and Valium
Cognitive therapy	Challenge false beliefs and assumptions
Cognitive-behavior therapy	Change thoughts and actions together; includes rational emotive behavior therapy
Electroconvulsive therapy	Use of electrical shocks to treat severe mental illness
Exposure therapy	Acclimation to fear-inducing stimuli
Free association	Report all thoughts that enter one's consciousness
Lobotomy	Surgical disconnection of nerves between frontal lobes and emotion-controlling areas of the brain
Progressive muscle relaxation	Sequential tightening and relaxing of muscles
Tardive dyskinesia	Involuntary movement of face and limbs
Transference	Relating therapist to authoritative figure

PSYCHOPATHOLOGY BREAKDOWN

Abnormality	Deviance, dysfunction, danger, distress
Anxiety disorders	Intense and persistent worry; generalized anxiety disorder, panic disorder, phobias, obsessive-compulsive disorder, posttraumatic stress disorder
Delusions	Unchangeable false beliefs
Dissociative disorders	Loss of memory and identity; dissociative identity disorder, dissociative amnesia, dissociative fugue
Eating disorders	Irrational beliefs about healthy weight and food consumption
Hallucinations	Vividly imagined auditory or visual sensations
Mood disorders	Emotional extremes; major depressive disorder and bipolar disorder
Organic disorders	Psychological problems caused by brain damage or chemical imbalance; dementia, Alzheimer's disease
Personality disorders	Persistent behavioral patterns that cause impaired social functioning
Schizophrenia	Split from reality, including delusions, hallucinations, disorganized thoughts, and inappropriate emotions
Somatoform disorders	Physical complaints without medical causes; conversion disorder, hypochondriasis, factitious disorders

10 SIGNIFICANT STUDIES

Ainsworth's strange situation	Placed infants in a novel environment and examined styles of attachment to parents
Asch's conformity experiment	In groups of three or more, people respond incorrectly to basic questions to fit in
Bandura's Bobo doll study	Children who watch aggressive adult models are more likely to behave aggressively
Harlow's monkey study	Monkeys are more likely to attach to warm, soft (fake) mothers than wire mothers who provide food
Kohler's study of insight learning	Observed chimpanzees learning how to reach bananas placed out of reach
Milgram's obedience study	Participants were willing to shock others, possibly to death, when instructed by an authority figure; demonstrated power of obedience
Pavlov's salivating dogs	Russian doctor studying digestion discovered operant conditioning when dogs began salivating in anticipation of food
Rosenhan's study of mental illness	Faked schizophrenia to receive admittance into mental hospital; realized that all actions were evaluated based on his diagnosis
Watson's Little Albert study	Classically conditioned fear of rats in a baby by pairing them with loud noises
Zimbardo's prison study	People were given roles of either prisoner or guard; participants took roles too far, and guards became abusive to prisoners

FINAL TIPS AND ABOUT THE AUTHOR

FINAL TIPS

- Cram study time in whenever you can: between class periods, while you are eating breakfast or brushing your teeth, during television commercials
- Use whatever study strategies work best for you: take notes, read out loud, scribble notes and drawings on a white board, or make up a story!
- Maximize the effectiveness of your study time by focusing most on the content areas that cover the largest percentage of the test
- Make sure you are well rested and well fed before the exam so that you have plenty of testing stamina
- Keep your energy high and your anxiety low
- Remember the principle of self-efficacy: if you are confident in your ability to succeed, you are more likely to meet those expectations!

ABOUT THE AUTHOR

Melanie Goodman is a caffeine-powered graduate student. Not long ago, she was a caffeine-powered AP test taker. In 2008, she graduated with a B.A. in Psychology at **Elmira College** and then moved to North Dakota to pursue a Ph.D. in clinical psychology. However, she discovered that -40° temperatures can induce psychosis. She now resides in California, where she studies education at California State University Northridge and practices operant conditioning with her Weimaraner puppy.

ABOUT THE EDITOR

DEAN SCHAFFER

Since leading Los Angeles's Taft High School to a national Academic Decathlon championship and shipping off to Stanford University, Dean Schaffer has designed and developed DemiDec's signature Power Guides and Cram Kits. Over the years, he has maintained his affinity for a variety of metaphorical hats (editing, writing, and layout, especially), non-metaphorical sunglasses (Aviators, always), and the guitar (Fender, usually). When he's not editing, Dean is generally looking for something nearby to edit— dont we all luv to find speling erors?

In his spare time, Dean ponders whether he'll ever be able to handle the luxury of spare time; luckily, he avoids this metaphysical quandary altogether by choosing not to affiliate himself with relaxation of any form. Instead, he occupies himself with songwriting, playing guitar, and parallel structure-ing. When he isn't doing those things, he's considering the merits of democratic elections, oligarchic disinterestedness, and delicious gouda cheese.

ABOUT DEMIDEC

THE DEMIDEC STORY

Since 1994, DemiDec has been the worldwide leader in student-centered learning experiences, from its curriculum for the Academic Decathlon in the United States to its college prep academies in Asia. DemiDec now brings its unique approach—and its mascot, the alpaca—to a whole new realm: AP and SAT materials.

To learn more, visit www.demidec.com.

ABOUT THE WORLD SCHOLAR'S CUP

Six subjects. Four events. Teams of three.

DemiDec's World Scholar's Cup is an international team academic tournament with thousands of participants in 30 countries. It centers on a different theme each year— from the Frontier to the Fall of Empires. Events include team debate, a scholar's bowl, and more.

Discover this year's theme, learn more about the program, and sign up for free at www.scholarscup.org.